Psychoanalytic Psychotherapy of the Severely Disturbed Adolescent

EFPP

The EFPP Clinical Monograph Series

Editor-in-Chief: *John Tsiantis*

Associate Editors: *Brian Martindale* (Adult Section)

Didier Houzel (Child & Adolescent Section)

Alessandro Bruni (Group Section)

OTHER MONOGRAPHS IN THE SERIES

- *Countertransference in Psychoanalytic Psychotherapy with Children and Adolescents*
- *Supervision and Its Vicissitudes*
- *Psychoanalytic Psychotherapy in Institutional Settings*

Psychoanalytic Psychotherapy of the Severely Disturbed Adolescent

edited by

Dimitris Anastasopoulos

SENIOR EDITOR

Effie Laylou-Lignos

Margot Waddell

Foreword by

Dimitris Anastasopoulos

published by

KARNAC BOOKS

for

The European Federation
for Psychoanalytic Psychotherapy
in the Public Health Services

First published in 1999 by
H. Karnac (Books) Ltd.
58 Gloucester Road
London SW7 4QY

British Library Cataloguing in Publication Data

A C.I.P. record for this book is available from the British Library.

ISBN 1-85575-214-X

Edited, designed, and produced by Communication Crafts

Printed in Great Britain by Polestar Wheatons Ltd, Exeter

10 9 8 7 6 5 4 3 2 1

ACKNOWLEDGEMENTS

I feel that it is a privilege to be the Senior Editor of a volume concerning the emotional disturbances of adolescents. The whole process towards the making of this book together with all those who have contributed in it was an enriching learning experience for me.

First of all, I would like to express my thanks to the contributors of this volume, who have kindly offered to share their experienced and creative work with us.

I also wish to express my gratitude to the Editor-in-Chief of the EFPP Monograph Series, John Tsiantis, for his endless encouragement and help during the editorial work. I would also like to thank deeply my co-editors Margot Waddell and Effie Laylou-Lignos for the active and immensely helpful support they gave me, all the way through the completion of this book.

Finally, I would like to express my special thanks to Philippa Martindale, who has patiently and efficiently edited the Monograph's material, to Penny Nikolaidou for her secretarial assistance, and, of course, to Cesare Sacerdoti, the publisher of the series.

Dimitris Anastasopoulos
Athens, August 1999

ABOUT THE AUTHORS

DIMITRIS ANASTASOPOULOS (Greece), MD, is an Adult and Child Psychiatrist working in Athens. He was trained in adolescent psychiatry and psychotherapy at the Tavistock Clinic, London, and he is a training psychotherapist for adult and adolescent psychotherapists in Greece. He is a member of the Executive Committee of the Hellenic Association of Child and Adolescent Psychoanalytic Psychotherapy (H.A.C.A.P.P.).

ROBIN ANDERSON (United Kingdom) is a Child and Adolescent Psychiatrist and is the Chairman of the Adolescent Department at the Tavistock Clinic. He is a Training Analyst in Child and Adult Analysis at the Institute of Psycho-Analysis, London.

HÉLÈNE DUBINSKY (United Kingdom) is a Consultant Child and Adolescent Psychotherapist in the Adolescent Department of the Tavistock Clinic in London. She is also an Adult Psychotherapist. Her particular interest lies in psychoanalytic psychotherapy with borderline adolescents and in brief interventions with young people. She has contributed to a number of books in different areas of therapeutic work with children and adolescents.

ALAIN GIBEAULT (France), PhD, is a Training Analyst of the Paris Psychoanalytic Society, President of the European Psychoanalytic Federation, and Director of the E. & J. Kestemberg Center (Mental Health Association of the 13th Arrondissement of Paris). He is the author of many papers on symbolization, regression, hypochondria, psychodrama, and graphic representations in prehistory.

PHILIPPE JEAMMET (France) is Professor of Child and Adolescent Psychiatry at the University of Paris, VI. He is Head of the Department of Adolescent and Young Adult Psychiatry at the Institut Mutualiste Montsouris in Paris. He is Psychoanalyst and Member of the Société Psychanalytique de Paris and the Honorary President of the International Society for Adolescent Psychiatry.

GIANLUIGI MONNIELLO (Italy), MD, is a Child Psychiatrist and Psychotherapist and is Head of the Day Hospital for adolescent patients in the Child and Adolescent Psychiatric Institute, University of Rome. He is the regional Vice-President, Italy, of the International Society for Adolescent Psychiatry. He is the Secretary for the Rome Association for Adolescent Psychotherapy.

ARNALDO NOVELLETTO (Italy), MD, is Associate Professor of Child and Adolescent Psychiatry at the University of Rome. He is a Full Member, Training and Supervising Analyst for the Italian Psychoanalytical Society. He was formerly the regional Vice-President of the International Society for Adolescent Psychiatry and President of the Rome Association for Adolescent Psychotherapy. He is the author of *Adolescent Psychoanalytic Psychiatry* and the editor of *Adolescence and Perversion; Adolescence, Love, Coupling; Adolescence and Trauma; Separation and Loneliness in Adolescence*—all published by Borla, Rome.

JULIA PESTALOZZI (Switzerland), M.B.B.S.(London), MD, trained as a clinical psychologist in Hungary and as a medical doctor in England. She specialized in psychiatry and psychotherapy for children and adolescents in Switzerland. She works in Basel as a Psychoanalyst, Psychotherapist, and Supervisor in private practice. Her main interest lies in the field of psychoanalytic psychotherapy of schizophrenias, particularly of adolescents. She is the Swiss delegate of the EFPP (Adult Section).

MARGOT WADDELL (United Kingdom) took a Doctorate in English Literature at Cambridge University before training as a Child Psychotherapist at the Tavistock Clinic, London. She is also an Associate Member of the British Psycho-Analytical Society and Consultant Child Psychotherapist in the Adolescent Department at the Tavistock Clinic. Her latest book, *Inside Lives: Psychoanalysis and the Growth of the Personality*, has just been published by Duckworth.

CONTENTS

FOREWORD

Dimitris Anastasopoulos

Let's go together, my friend
even if they are stoning us;
let them say we are riding the air
all those that have never felt
from what kind of iron, stones, blood and fire
we are built, dream and sing.

Odysseas Elytis, *Sun the First*, XVI

Adolescence as a transitional psychic process is universally accepted. The description given by Aristotle of the young people of the fourth century BC contains observations that are still applicable to the adolescents of today. However, it was not until comparatively recently that the particular requirements and phenomena of adolescent psychopathology and of the therapeutic approach to them began to be of concern to professionals. Psychotherapy with adolescents—especially with severely disturbed adolescents—is a demanding and challenging procedure, full of unexpected events and fluctuations in the pace of progress, in which stages in development become interwoven with strong emotions of transference and countertransference.

We know that it is natural for adolescents to give the appearance of being unsettled and unpredictable, oscillating between extreme positions. An emotional disturbance can prevent or inhibit the gradual psychological integration of the adolescent towards adulthood. Psychotherapy is called upon to restore the continuity and dynamics of the development which has been interrupted, stabilizing the ego and the self-image and promoting more mature identification. Psychotherapists must be significantly skilled in containing the anxiety and massive projections of adolescence, and they must also possess the flexibility that will enable them to respond to shifts and variations in level of development and severity of regression.

I myself tend to view each psychotherapy with an adolescent as a process in which therapist and patient are attempting to direct themselves towards a kind of regeneration, in which they proceed along the wire like acrobats, with no safety net. I believe that a successful psychotherapy requires controlled psychic fusion through the repeated projective and introjective identifications of the adolescent with the therapist. The therapist's ability to participate, to feel, and to contain is, perhaps, the ultimate requirement in this process.

The importance of the theme of this volume needs no further explanation. As a "second chance"—to use Blos's term—adolescence contains components that are capable of leading either to the restoration of the fragmented personality or to a hell in which a chaotic psychic disturbance becomes permanent. This volume brings together a distillation of the therapeutic experience and thinking of senior psychoanalytic therapists working in different European countries and belonging to different "schools" of psychoanalysis. I believe that it will contribute to the exploration of the therapeutic approach to severely disturbed adolescents which has got under way in recent years. The cross-cultural nature of the book is, in particular, a symbol of the prospect of a Europe without frontiers and of the development of the theoretical basis and clinical practice of psychoanalytic psychotherapy beyond ideological classifications and obstacles. That, I believe, was also the purpose of the foundation and operation of the EFPP.

INTRODUCTION

Robin Anderson

Adolescent disturbance has in recent years become a major preoccupation in Western society. Young people are often seen as a danger to the adult world, with their violent behaviour, crime, and soccer hooliganism and their dangerous sexuality, or as a source of worried preoccupation and concern about their vulnerability to drug abuse, homelessness, and unemployment. These concerns, though they also reflect the projected fears of the adult world, do, I think, have a basis in reality.

Jeammet in chapter two emphasizes the constant interaction between the individual, the family, and society, where disturbance in one is always seen in the other. Society is indeed dealing with change which seems to be occurring at an ever faster pace. From the point of view of social cohesiveness, the most significant changes are probably those caused by the increasing mobility of families where traditional patterns of employment have been lost, with the result that families have to move in search of work. As a consequence, there is an increasing reliance on the nuclear family and a corresponding loss of the influence and support of the extended family. Nuclear families, too, are different. They are often no longer permanent units in which children could be expected to be living with both parents throughout their childhood. Now a large proportion of parents separate at least once while their children are growing up, and the latter are then often brought up by one parent, usually the mother either on her own or in a relationship with a new partner.

These changes affect adolescents in all strata of society. A recent British survey showed that drug use was in fact more common in middle-class young people. However, the most vulnerable adolescents are to be found in the most deprived parts of society, where the weakened role and status of fathers—often long-term unemployed—adds to the general instability.

It is in this context that adolescent development is taking place. The problem for adolescents and those caring for them is that this fundamental period of change and transition is massive and creates anxieties that need to be contained. It is when the anxiety cannot be contained, because of either internal or external failure, that we see disturbance and breakdown.

After infancy, adolescence is probably the period where the most fundamental changes take place, over a period of only a few years. Ushered in by puberty, it starts with young people being faced with a surge of physical developments that all have to be emotionally processed. These hormonal increases themselves produce surges of sexual feelings as well as giving rise to all the primary and secondary effects of puberty. The young person therefore is required to adapt to alterations of size, shape, and build and to changes in strength, in appearance, in the sound of the voice, and in being sexually mature—and so for boys to be able to impregnate, or for girls to have a baby. Both internal and external pressures require the development of the capacity to become intimate with others and to form sexual relationships, to become less dependent on parents, and to move towards separation from the family. In the modern world, substantial educational achievements are also expected, and in this time of enormous upheavals in the world of work, the need to be more educated increases this pressure on young people. In other words, no sphere of life is untouched.

There is a rapid change of perspective which leaves the adolescent with a completely new sense of what the world is like and what he or she is like in the world. Yet there is a paradox that will be familiar to all who work psychoanalytically. This adult body and adult world, which are both thrust at the young person and sought by them, in no way eclipses the infant self and its desires and fears. Thus these massive changes and re-orientations that assault the personality create tremendous tension. This new physical equipment and this increase of potency are essential to allow the young person to function as an adult, but they are also the means to gratify infantile wishes—both sexual and destructive—which may still be very strong so that the combination of intense irrational desires with greater power can seem, and even be, dangerous. A small boy involved in a classic oedipal conflict may want to kill his father and he may attempt to enact this, but he lacks both the strength and cognitive capacity to put this into effect. His father can quite easily prevent any harm, and an episode such as a temper tantrum can usually pass without too much residual anxiety. It is the very balance of a relatively weak child and relatively strong parents which, whatever the impulses and anxieties, is a background bedrock of reality which allows for a sense of safety. In adolescence, the situation is extremely different. The boy is suddenly quite strong and with more cognitive capacity, and he could kill his father if he did not prevent himself, and yet the impulse may be just as strong or, with the hormonal enhancement of the emotional state, even stronger. The result may be that a situation can develop in which there is either real danger or more usually great anxiety about a danger, arising both within the adolescent and in those caring for him.

These kinds of anxieties are generated in connection with sexual as well as destructive impulses (and are often a mutually enhancing combination of the two). A young man of 18 was referred to me in a very anxious state, afraid that he was going mad. He was suddenly terrified of the thought that if he wished he could kill his girlfriend. On another occasion he had the thought that he could make sexual advances on his mother. Fortunately, in his case, there was enough of a bedrock of stability to prevent him from acting these out, but there were very unresolved issues in relation to his parents which had emerged during his childhood when his father had left him and his mother. The patient had not dealt sufficiently with his oedipal rivalry with his father as a child, and when this re-erupted in adolescence he had to cope with some powerful early anxieties but now in the much more dangerous context of an adult world and in an adult body.

Most children achieve some kind of stability of personality by the time they reach adolescence, but it is a stability that occurs in the context of a relatively static internal and external world. Adolescence sweeps all this away, and the adjustment must now be achieved in the context of continuous change. Anastasopoulos (chapter three) describes adolescence as a series of "psychic ruptures and disorganizations" even "traumas" that place demands for adjustment on the young person which stretches his or her capacities more than ever before. The difference between pre- and post-adolescence can be likened to the difference between finding one's balance whilst standing still and finding it whilst in motion. The enthusiasm with which many adolescents take up roller-blading or BMX cycling seems to capture this need to master the world of instability and change.

It is in this way that we can see how, despite earlier failures of development, fixations, or aberrant adjustments, it may have been possible to achieve a kind of stability in childhood that nonetheless leaves the personality insufficiently resilient to cope with the pressures of adolescence, and it is at this time that the massive increase in manifest disturbance occurs. Thus Novelletto and Monniello (chapter five) write: "The oedipal conflict, both when it first arises and upon its post-puberty re-enactment, is the acid test that can throw the narcissistic structure of the self into crisis." They point out that the resulting disturbance can occur in a variety of ways according to the fault lines already existing in the personality. Indeed, the emphasis from nearly all the contributors to this book is that the more fundamental or the earlier the failure of integration, the more serious will be the disturbance in adolescent breakdown. It is these kinds of patients that the contributors are considering.

Margot Waddell (chapter one) describes how the unsound adjustments based largely on projective mechanisms can lead to a series of borrowed identities that often do not serve the personality sufficiently well to allow the young person to pass through adolescence without breaking down. She contrasts this to surer identifications that she sees as being based more on introjective processes.

The kinds of adolescents that this book is addressing not only break down more seriously and fundamentally, but they pose greater problems in management and treatment than is the case with younger, and often also with older, patients. It is widely recognized that it is almost the norm for adolescents to deal with their conflicts by action. The more primitive and violent the conflicts, the more likely they are to be enacted in the immediate environment. The alpha process that in infancy mainly took place between a baby and a mother now takes place with the wider family, schoolteachers, the police, the criminal courts, and so forth. Projective processes are to the fore, and when breakdown occurs it is often because either these are too great or too powerful or because the containing structures are too impaired to cope.

Sometimes it is possible, even in this anxious climate, to improve the level of containment sufficiently and to engage analytically with the young person to allow a de-escalation of the projective processes and for treatment to begin to improve the situation. This kind of approach is more possible in centres specializing in the treatment of young people where adolescent psychotherapy with psychiatric support and good liaison can provide a holding structure. This kind of approach allowed the treatment of Hélène Dubinsky's (chapter seven) very disturbed patients, including one with a full-blown schizophrenic illness, to take place. In the United Kingdom, in addition to the Tavistock Clinic such specialist services as the Brent Adolescent Centre and the Portman Clinic do manage to treat quite ill adolescent patients on an out-patient basis.

However, there are many circumstances where this is not possible. Either the necessary support from the family or the community is not there, or the young person is too disturbed, too at risk, or even too dangerous to remain in the community. Sometimes it is a combination of a level of risk that is too great together with a young person who cannot on his own manage the gaps between sessions without resorting to risky acting out as well as attending very erratically.* Many of the contributors are writing from the perspective of these patients.

Thus Novelletto and Monniello (chapter five) provide psychoanalytic work with young people who are detained for violent crimes. They convey how a destructive act can form a milestone in the decline of a young person who is perhaps heading towards a life-cycle of crime and punishment. However, the physical detention can be used to provide a structure for psychoanalytic psychotherapy in which a criminal act can be given meaning for the young person. One of their examples shows beautifully how the judge in one young man's mind changes, over the course of the few months that he is waiting for his trial, from a harsh and rigid superego, who administers death as the only response to wrongdoing, to a discriminating figure who is able to respond appropriately to what was a serious violent crime (this was how the judge appeared in a dream that the young man had a few days before his trial). They write of how the patient is able to move from a position where "What is clear, in short, is his hesitant attempt at separation from an original maternal object that cannot be explored, known, modulated, where there is no possibility of negotiation but only an absolute answer: life or death", to one in which the patient had moved to a situation in which the object could now be felt to have discrimination, thoughtfulness, and understanding. Firm, yes, but also fair, not the murderous superego inherited from his parents.

I suspect that these young people in prison awaiting trial have something in common with Anastasopoulos's patients (chapter three): they have created a traumatic situation (for themselves as well as for their victims). The help offered does seem to provide some of them with the opportunity for working through earlier conflicts, and the chapter provides a convincing case for such work to be made more available to this significant group of young people who otherwise themselves become increasingly damaged as well as damaging to society.

---

*For simplicity, in general discussions we have used the masculine pronouns for patients and the feminine pronouns for therapists.

This problem of engaging with adolescent patients—or indeed of having a patient to engage with—brings to mind the dictum of Mrs Beeton, the writer of a famous nineteenth-century English cookbook, whose recipe for jugged hare begins with the statement: "First catch your hare." This problem, so clearly illustrated by Novelletto and Monniello in the context of young people being held in prison, can in non-criminal situations be dealt with, for some patients, by admission to hospital where psychotherapy can then take place in a supportive and safe environment. However, even in an in-patient setting some young people just cannot engage. Jeammet, in his chapter "Links between Internal and External Reality in Devising a Therapeutic Setting for Adolescents Who Present with Serious Conduct Disorders" (chapter two), addresses this issue as part of a detailed discussion of narcissistic disorders. Many young people with narcissistic disorders cannot deal with the conflict that arises when they are in analytic treatment. They may retreat from it or refuse to take part in it. For many of these patients, the fear of regression to unmodified infantile states is too terrifying. This kind of personality structure is present in many severely disturbed young people, and even in an in-patient setting this poses a serious therapeutic challenge. In both Jeammet's chapter and that of Alain Gibeault ("An Invitation to a Journey: The Function of the Double in the Psychoanalytic Psychodrama of a Psychotic Adolescent", chapter six), a very particular type of psychodrama is used in which a young person has sessions with a number of therapists who help him to play out and face his anxieties. These authors have found, as they illustrate very clearly, how even frozen and withdrawn young people can tentatively allow themselves to take part in an event that does not intrude into them but goes on in their presence. Gibeault shows in his illustration of a pre-adolescent boy how the boy's involvement in the process was possible by literally making a leap from the sidelines into a world of play and imagination, and by doing so he had allowed himself to face fears of dying. Both Jeammet and Gibeault show how this kind of invitation to be involved proved irresistible in two very withdrawn patients, and once engaged they could then gain confidence that they would not be harmed by their contact with a therapeutic process.

Pestalozzi (chapter four), in a very beautiful clinical account of a dysmorphophobic boy, describes how she was able to slowly make contact in a way that showed great sensitivity for his psychotic defences so that he could begin to trust her and so find other less destructive ways of managing his emotional state. The accounts of Dubinsky (chapter seven) and Waddell (chapter one) also show how, with some kinds of fragile patients, a slow and careful technique that does not push them faster than they can go can begin to help even quite disturbed patients, in whom psychotic processes have become the dominant force in the personality, to be helped with out-patient psychotherapy.

Anastasopoulos (chapter three) looks at a very particular but common precipitant of disturbance in adolescents, that of trauma. Often, under circumstances of a trauma, adolescents can present with signs of very severe disturbance. Some seem to respond well to even relatively short periods of help, whereas for others the trauma seems to be the start of a process that is much more intractable. Anastasopolous, through some careful clinical illustrations, shows very convincingly that those who have arrived at adolescence with earlier conflicts sufficiently worked through can, even though they may appear very disturbed, respond well to quite limited help, whilst those for whom the trauma came after earlier childhood trauma, or with other unresolved conflicts, require much more help.

These chapters are written by psychoanalytic psychotherapists from different countries of Europe and from different analytic traditions, and yet it can be seen that there is a thread running through all of them which shows that our common psychoanalytic ancestry has interacted creatively with our different traditions in Europe. Sometimes these seem to divide us, but I think that they can also be shown to enrich us as we face a common and serious challenge to our psychoanalytic skills and to the future adults of Europe.

Psychoanalytic Psychotherapy of the Severely Disturbed Adolescent

CHAPTER ONE

A mind of one's own: introjective processes and the capacity to think

Margot Waddell

Establishing an identity is a central task for adolescents—discovering who one is, finding a mind of one's own—an internal analogue to the room that Virginia Woolf (1928) designates as essential not only to the capacity to create, but to the possibility of "living in the presence of reality" (p. 109). How does the internal room become structured and furnished in its own unique and idiosyncratic way—not as a prefab, identikit, design-catalogue sort of room, but as a space of one's own?

"A mind of his own" was what "Tom"—a college student in his first year—most wanted. Although when he started treatment he was chronologically a young man, in fact he seemed locked in an entrenched and protracted adolescent state of mind from which he felt unable to emerge. Of medium stature and strongly built, with dark, prematurely receding hair, he could, at times, be strikingly good-looking. This was not a view he shared. Tremendously sensitive to his appearance, his loss of hair was a source of

---

This chapter was originally given as a lecture to a mixed professional and non-professional audience, autumn, 1995.

constant anguish; it was a narcissistic affront, fuelled by the relentlessly cruel jokes of his hard-drinking "macho" friends.

His culture was typically adolescent, in the pejorative sense. It was group-orientated and predominantly mindless and aimless, though not without some mutually supportive qualities. His own life featured slavish attention to physical appearance: excessive drinking bouts at pubs (alcohol having succeeded the extensive drug-taking of his early teens); states of languid and mawkish self-pity, alternating with energetic and competitive sportiness; periods of, by turn, obsessive philosophical and political ruminations and manic excitability. Like his friends, he had become a chronic under-achiever and had exiled himself from his professional middle-class upbringing to join an "underclass" mentality. The only preoccupations that were not group-orientated were his erotic fantasies and, at times, activities. These were kept frantically secret, with enormous shame attached to the risk of discovery.

In the early months he described, scarcely coherently, his inability to think for himself or to concentrate. His mind was continuously filled with perverse sexual fantasies. He spent most of his time in a frenzied, masturbatory state of excitement, using sex-phone-lines and calls to prostitutes. He had only recently stopped exposing himself to women in parklands and open spaces. He was a late university entrant. He had left school at age 15 and worked as a builder and as a painter-decorator, beginning A-level evening classes when he was 18. He was born out of wedlock, and his parents never lived together. His father, a writer of some repute, has remained in sporadic contact with him over the years. His mother had married and left her country of origin to come to England with Tom when he was 4 years old.

This marriage seems to have constituted a major blow to Tom at the time, and subsequently it deteriorated into sado-masochistic misery. His stepfather was experienced as a tyrant and a bully. Alcoholic and morose, he would dictate rules to the household, and to Tom in particular, of peevish triviality, relating with a sort of dour imperviousness to any joyfulness or finer feeling. Tom hated him.

Shortly after the birth of a second son, two years after the marriage, Tom's mother had a full puerperal breakdown, which initiated a chronic schizophrenic illness. Despite conscious idealization of his earliest years alone with his mother, it seemed more likely, in the light of his subsequent difficulties, that even this early "idyll" was shadowed by maternal depression. From the transference could be inferred an experience of a mind unreceptive and unresponsive to Tom's projections and communications. There would seem to have been an absence of vitality, thoughtfulness, interest, or hope of the kind that might have enabled him to feel understood, and from which he could have derived a sense of himself and internalized a capacity to think for himself. Indeed, his extreme difficulty in "thinking" at all, in the sense that I have been describing, suggests that he had experienced so little containment in infancy, particularly of his sadistic and aggressive impulses, that a good object would almost have to be "constructed" *for* him—by way, initially, of thinking for him and then, only slowly, with him. He alternated between a fear of being merged with his object and that of being totally cut off from it. Either way he was unable consciously to think.

In the literal sense, Tom did have a room of his own. I often heard about it, together with his attendant longing that I might actually see it. He believed that were I to do so, I would then understand him, for every square inch of wall and door was covered with memorabilia—fragments, representations, relics, reminders of past events. The memorabilia offered recollections of experiences, relationships, and exchanges dating from early days at primary school, through his travels abroad, his chance encounters, and his important relationships, to the present day. There were photos, postcards, bus tickets, labels, letters, matchboxes, concert tickets, napkins, notes, stamps, every imaginable object that could be stuck to a surface. To know his room, he insisted, was to know him. In a sense he was right, for what the room demonstrated was his belief that these multifarious images of himself amounted to an identity.

The room represented, rather, an agglomeration of disparate and discrete bits and pieces, many of them filched or stolen odds-and-ends—a sort of potpourri of a life, about which it was, in fact, impossible to think. There existed a mistaken notion that this accumulation of detail, with its strong, quantitative, and scavenging emphasis, had something to do with identity. But it felt like a stolen identity. There was an exoskeletal sense of serial accretions, with adhesive and projective characteristics, in essence narcissistic, based in the recollection of a face or event, in contrast to an introjection of that face or event such that they might "exist in the mind", alive and independent of one's self and will. He had a physical room, then, but no mind/room of his own—no internal place where meaning might be generated, no secure relationship with constant and developing objects, as opposed to the shifting insignificance of ephemera.

The capacity to construct internally a room of one's own is based in the experience of having had "room to think"—an experience located from the beginning in the matrix of relations between mother and infant. Wilfred Bion (1962a, 1962b) describes that thinking as a function that, initially, the mother's internal object performs for the baby—drawing on her capacity to experience her infant unconsciously as well as consciously. In good circumstances she is able, in a state of reverie, to take in communications that the infant, himself or herself, is not yet able to understand. In making sense of them, she enables the baby slowly to acquire the internal resources to think about experience and thereby to render it meaningful. This capacity to "hold" or "contain" the baby's states of mind is dependent on the mother being able to be continent and cognisant of her own mental states, neither intruding them into her infant nor presenting an unreceptive surface to the infant's projections and efforts to communicate.

Central to Bion's contribution was the notion that the vicissitudes of embryonic thought lie at the heart of psychic development. The essential question becomes one of what kind of thinking is going on and how it links to emotional, in contrast to merely cognitive, processes. To the more familiar conflict between Love (L) and Hate (H), Bion added that between Knowledge (K)—or the desire to understand—and aversion to knowing and understanding, as fundamental to the personality's capacity to grow. It is in the course of adolescence that the battle between L, H, and K on the one hand, and their converse—the negative grid of –L, –H, and –K—are often violently and, in terms of the ultimate outcome for the personality, crucially fought (1962a, pp. 42–49; 1963, pp. 51–53). For learning about oneself can be a very painful process. "'[T]hey' all hate learning", says the psychoanalyst in Bion's final

Memoir, "It makes them develop—swell up" (1979, p. 438)—pregnant, that is, with a new idea, a new birth/thought in the mind. F. Scott Fitzgerald put it another way: "I was impelled to think, God, was it difficult! The moving about of great secret trunks." It is the capacity to think about emotional experiences, to engage with them, suffer them, which feeds the mind and promotes growth—a capacity constantly opposed by intolerance of frustration and of the pain of emotions.

In essence, the process of acquiring a mind of one's own, so that it is possible to think about emotional experiences, involves the shedding of defensive, look-alike characteristics (abandoning adhesive modes and moving out of projective identification would be one way of putting it) and identifying with good objects—primarily, perhaps, with an awareness of, and an engagement with, what might be called a good internal couple. The creative capacity of this couple may be felt to be such that a space is offered for the development of the embryo-mind, so that it can become itself, deformed neither by internal narcissistic identifications on the one hand, nor by external intrusions on the other. This is what is meant here by introjective identification, a process whereby over time the baby, or patient, has the opportunity for, and acquires the capacity to take in and then draw on, supportive and loving experiences that safeguard, protect, and inspire the growing personality.

It is important to dwell for a moment on the specificity of the kind of introjective process being described, for it represents a very distinct emphasis within introjective processes more generally. The kind of introjection drawn on here could be said to lie at the core of development, inseparable from a capacity for intimacy, with its implications of differentiation and separation—two of the most important tasks of late adolescence. A difference has to be established, in other words, between the all too readily made, indeed ready-made, identifications—immediate ones (especially in adolescence) or perhaps lasting ones—with bad internal or external objects (or part objects) and bad parts of the self, and a contrasting and much more positive kind of identification, with the qualities and functions of a good object or objects, particularly with an internal mature parental couple. It has been suggested that this latter kind of identification, on which the adult part of the personality is premised—is resourced by truth-telling as a mode and sincerity as an emotional stance. Donald Meltzer (1978) has called this introjection "the most important and most mysterious concept in psychoanalysis" (p. 459). This mode of identification is marked by a capacity to bear uncertainty and not-knowing, by contrast with an irritable reaching after fact and reason—as Keats (1817) puts it in his notion of Negative Capability (*Letters*, p. 43). It distinguishes what it means really to be grown up from the predominantly adhesive and projective states that tend to characterize adolescent struggles and may masquerade as "grown-up". Meltzer describes how elements of the experience of sense-of-identity that relate to this kind of introjective identification have a prospective quality, an aspirational tone, that is quite different from the immediate and delusional self-feeling produced by projective identification. "Tentativeness, humility, self doubt, and like nuances of emotion, therefore attach to these aspects of the sense-of-identity and make up the shadings of a person's character that most impress us as sincere" (1971, p. 205). It is the phenomenology of this mode of introjective identification which may help in thinking about Tom's coming-to-be, or coming-to-have a mind of his own.

Dream images of different houses and rooms, being built or decorated, permeated Tom's analysis in a fascinating way. His ever-changing dream experiences of these spaces charted his relationship to the analysis and to me: by turn spoiling with shoddy work; trying to cut corners and get away with it; overcharging; undercharging; desperately trying to make progress yet finding himself delaying or malingering; blaming bad work on other workmen; taking responsibility for mistakes; discovering false walls with a succession of hidden rooms still to be worked on; spilling paint and destroying the carpet; staining; repairing; and so on.

A brief, early dream encapsulates his ongoing struggle in the transference to experience me in terms that Bion might regard as a "thinking breast", one that could offer the mental and emotional structure that Tom needed in order to begin developing. *He was trying to play tennis on an indoor court. There were two problems: not only was one wall of the court missing, but every time he threw the ball up to serve, it hit an unnaturally low ceiling and bounced back at him, making it impossible to start playing.*

This dream, and others like it, would seem to describe a very early experience in which something in the containing structure was felt to be missing. So, too, in the transference, I was felt either to be unwilling or unable to receive his communications. Yet were I to do so, I would be put in danger of being driven mad by them in just the way that he feared his mother had been incapable of withstanding the toxicity of his projections. We might conjecture that, as a baby, each time he attempted to project his feelings with the hope that, once received, the processes of projection and introjection might be set in play, a blank, wall-eyed expression in his mother's face and mind (the unnaturally low ceiling) bounced his feelings back at him, leaving him both confused as to the meaning of his experience and as to the dysjunction between what he thought his eyes could see in his mother's face (or did they?) and the ugly feelings he was left with. Put another way, perhaps the unnaturally low ceiling prevented Tom discovering that something fundamental was missing and that, should he succeed in serving something up, and projecting it, that "something" would end in outer space. How could he construe the meaning of the inside from the contours of the outside? One defensive manoeuvre was to become, literally, confused, so attached to this or that narcissistic identification that he was in a chronic muddle about the boundary between his mind and that of his object, between internal and external, self and other.

The adhesive qualities of the room/womb that he had constructed for himself externally seemed a very accurate representation of his internal state. Lacking an internal container of meaning, he had resorted to a kind of two-dimensionality—the sort of skin-container described by Bion (1962a) and Esther Bick (1968). His painful early experiences seemed to have left him completely unhoused, wholly ill-equipped to take the necessary developmental steps towards the acquisition of his own identity, rather than settling for someone who resembled a self, but who functioned more as a cardboard cutout figure than as a fully dimensional person. Tom described himself as forever propping up such a figure in front of himself, changing the appearance according to which group he was with at the time, an ever-shifting sense of identity. A scavenger himself, he assumed that others were too. "I open the door of my personality and let everyone in to take what they find, different things for each of them. But really, whatever the outside looks like, the inside is empty." He spoke with uncharacteristic coherence and insight. He felt himself to be a series of surfaces, with nothing real inside at all.

By the end of the first year, Tom was starting to "apprehend" (with fear and trepidation) the meaning of beginning to think, both the nature of the process and the risk that it posed to him. Just before the summer break he had the first of his train dreams: *he was at an underground station where the line was about to take a sort of loop. He was not sure whether to get the train there, or to catch it on the way back.* (Tom starts his journey to the clinic on the Piccadilly Line, and the "underground" comings and goings are recurrent features of his dreams, particularly in terms of expressing his orientation to the analytic process.) Tom's immediate thought about the dream was that it had something to do with his travelling to Heathrow the following day to go abroad for a holiday. There is indeed a loop in the line between terminals. His dream-predicament seemed to be to do with the danger of maintaining a train of thought in my absence (i.e. without me to hold him). If he kept me in mind as a continuation of his analysis, he would be having to keep his loopy-self in mind, with the danger of driving him round-the-bend. Would it be better, perhaps, to cut off completely and simply to get back on the train again on the way home? Or did this dream represent the possibility of maintaining mental continuity in my absence. I rather felt that "going on thinking" without an available container to hold the emotionality and render it bearable threatened him, at this point, with madness.

Some time before this, there had been a dream-image of bodies on a train track, with the implication, as we examined it, that "laying things on the line", managing to "think" them, to know them and name them, was death-dealing—a death, we might feel, that is a necessary part of any psychological birth. This was the measure of risk involved in the inception of the thinking process. It was one that, at the time, he hardly dared take. Indeed, for several months after that dream Tom withdrew into obsessive sexual ruminations, feeling that he had thoughts about which he dared not think. The "train of thought" metaphor was ambiguous: it expressed the capacity to sustain a thinking process in a creative and developmental mode, and also a notion of being trammelled, linear, and therefore limited to a narrative, "and then, and then, and then", mode (perhaps the difference between K and –K).

Tom's emergence, shortly before the summer break, from this rather mindless state was heralded by a dream of which the content, together with the nature of the responses to my comments, demonstrated both his struggle to be born as a "thinking being" and his aversion to it:

> *He was experiencing a kind of sickening pressure, a panic about having to make sense of something in a very short time. He was trying to write, but there was not enough time to get whatever it was down. He was unable to order things properly. He knew there were thoughts but he couldn't think them, could not give them shape or substance. Gradually it became clear that what he was trying to write about was the discovery of a man's body that had been confined in a wall and was being dug out. Astonishingly, the man was still alive. The facts seemed to indicate that there was a question of usurping—someone had taken his place in life, operating as some kind of peasant, revolutionary hero. The discovery that the man was still alive was going on in the very process of trying to think about it, and write about it—hence the confusion.*

I suggested that the struggle to write (i.e. to articulate the process symbolically and thus to give it meaning) might describe the struggle to think about the experience of being dug out of his walled-up mentality and emotionally fragile identity (just alive), one that had been usurped long ago by, in his case, look-alike "identities", and grandiose fantasies (not unlike his early adolescent daydreams of undifferentiated heroics, whether as part of the SAS or of some far-flung revolutionary cause). Coming alive would mean not so much a fantasied revolution but a real one, signalled by catastrophic anxiety. Pressurized by the impending break, he felt panicked by not having enough time with me to think things out and make sense of his experience.

My talking in these terms first evoked doubt in him about whether his dream narrative was true—that is, as he had dreamed it, or as he had described it: "maybe it wasn't like that?" This then aroused a violent impulse to say something dismissive and spiteful to me and, following that, to reach out a violent strangling hand towards me. The final destructive impulse felt to him like the urge, at times enacted as a child, to break up and stamp on his precious toys before his mother's horrified eyes—wanting to cut off and strangle my speech (the helping hand that is being refused) and break my thoughts into fragments. It was the impulse to destroy something that he deeply cared for. Nodding tearfully, he said, "I *am* worried about the break". Though long walled-up, the "real" self was alive, but being in contact with that self, that identity, rather than usurping it with heroic imitations, threatened disintegration. The fear of dependency, separation, and loss simply felt too overwhelming. Hamlet-like, he attempted to disorder or dismantle his thoughts through a range of moves, from doubting the analysis, amounting to falsification of the original narrative (perhaps it wasn't true), to cynicism, and eventually to destructive action.

A further dream, around the same time, described a similar process, one that was often to be repeated in the sessions themselves. Tom would struggle towards an experience of a thinking container of meaning in his relationship with me, only to leave it immediately, unable to stay with the experience itself.

> In the dream, *he reluctantly leaves behind a group of male, pub-drinking, football-playing friends. He travels up a mountain on a steep railway-track, with a female companion. Quite high up it becomes colder, and he notices a beautiful house. He wonders how it could have been constructed, how building materials could have been carried up there. Briefly he seems to be in the house itself, wandering around its spacious rooms, thinking about its structure and the fact that it seemed similar both to the house of his mother and stepfather, and also to that of his natural father and his partner, which he had on occasions visited. He wished that the house was his own, or that he could have such a home. The next moment he was back in the train, descending now, and finding himself with one of his pub friends, who told him that he* [my patient] *had won a $64,000 quiz prize: Excited, he waved the cheque around. On closer inspection, however, he be-*

came unsure as to whether the cheque was or was not for $64,000: perhaps it was for $600, or even $60, or maybe for nothing at all.

The dream was typical of holiday-break dreams to come. It graphically described the central importance of the comings and goings to the sessions by train. It also described recognition of the extreme difficulty of staying in the house/session/mind itself—the construction of which had so captured his imagination. Having left behind his basic-assumption-group–self, at the bottom of the hill (his group-orientated, posturing, conforming, anti-developmental self), the journey towards the psychic container takes him up to a place that he expects to be colder but also, perhaps, brighter and clearer. He can appreciate the structural qualities of the analytic/house/mind, and the evidence of its inner workings. Once in the house, however, he almost immediately finds himself embarking on a descent—suggesting the difficulty of staying with his object and going on thinking, rather than succumbing to an impulse to possess it, imitate it, or merely to envy it, which sets him back on a downhill path. Unable to bear the frustration of not having it, he finds that he has already lost the good experience. He is back on the train, leaving it behind. His state of mind degenerates further in the manic grandiosity of hitting the analytic jackpot: "winning" an answer to the $64,000 question, which would constitute a Eureka-type breakthrough experience (often quite consciously and explicitly longed for), without the hard work of engaging with the analytic relationship and with the pain of dependency and separation.

As soon as he had an inkling in the dream that there existed a house/mind that had an internal structure, one that had to be worked upon and was linked, somehow, with the function of parents, he began to think about how to construct such a building himself. But without yet having understood or experienced much of a sense of external or internal parenting—parents who could be allowed to work together for his welfare—he could not sustain it, and he gave way to envy and possibly to idealization. He certainly admires the house, internally supported as it is by paternal and maternal structures, but he is not able to respond to it or take it in. He is left with an impoverished conceptual framework. He enquires no further but moves back down the mountain, where he attempts to master feelings triumphantly, only to be left with doubts as to whether he can trust his senses and thus, finally, with feelings of emptiness and meaninglessness. The delusion of being the "winner" puts him back in a state of confusion.

It will be noted that the extensive travelling to and from the house/mind still takes up most of his emotional energy. The time actually spent in the house is very brief and scarcely connected to the journey. Nonetheless, I think that the house on the mountain does represent the "apprehension" of a thinking process, the beauty of which is inseparable from the anxiety and the hard work of constructing it in the inclement and cold conditions of the mind's struggle to change. There may certainly be some idealization of the house too, but I rather think that the dream indicates something of the perception of the truth on the one hand, and the urge to distort it on the other: the step-by-step process of a striving towards truthfulness (K) and the forces that are mobilized to counteract that (–K)—the forces that distort incipient thought (in this case, envy, idealization, omnipotence, and self-deception).

* * *

We can now jump forward two years, to Tom's approaching a particular developmental hurdle, one that so frequently proves the site of adolescent torment and breakdown—taking exams. He was understandably very anxious, for the previous year at exam-time he had got into a manic and persecuted state in which he had been unable to work and had had to ask for a deferment. It had seemed as if his recently acquired capacity to think things out and to write essays was feared to be of a projective and imitative kind (mainly in relation to me and a much admired tutor), and not one based in stable internal resources. He had been granted a time extension. Relieved of external pressure, the world had regained more ordinary proportions. But little light had been shed on the source of Tom's extreme panic. It felt as if issues had been shelved rather than resolved. Now, with finals looming, the already somewhat familiar disturbances again alerted us to impending danger. Tom had become much more articulate and clear-thinking about his experiences. He described his increasingly disturbed state of mind very graphically: his sense of total isolation in a corrupt and destructive world—a world in which it was vouchsafed to very few to share his nihilistic visions, probably, he thought, only to Ken Kesey, Doris Lessing, and Anthony Burgess. His ability to think or to concentrate again became minimal, and he lay locked in a panic of fragmentation and despair. He felt impelled to take on the mantle of a prophet of doom, planning to preach in the Underground that the end of the world was at hand, to harangue the Adam Smith Society, to stick bills, and to make speeches. The dreams that week made it clear that Tom felt that he had lost his way and needed me to lead him, only to find himself terrified that the boundary between his mind and mine had broken down, that he had induced me to be both mad like his mother, and brutal and tyrannical like his stepfather. At times he was able to articulate this clearly: "I am afraid that I will persuade you of my picture of the world—that that will get into you and you won't be able to tell me about what my mind is doing."

At the end of that week and the beginning of the next, it became possible to make some links between his exam panic and a number of hitherto unconscious determinants of his fear of success and his courting of failure. Two events prompted me to think about the degree of wilfulness and rage that were involved in Tom's seeming inability to bear being tested in this way. A telephone call from his mother enquiring when his graduation would take place, so that she could arrange her holiday accordingly, prompted a furious outburst from Tom: "Graduation—there won't be a graduation." His mother, thinking unusually coherently and thoughtfully on this occasion, had to be brutally punished.

He then described a dream in which *he was in a desperate panic about being late for a session with me. In order to reach me he had to cross a park where he kept being waylaid, having to walk around, or through, the various women's houses and gardens, which stood in his path.* This was the very park where he used to expose himself before analysis began. These other versions of me, whom he regularly sexualized in his erotic fantasies, diverted him from reaching the analyst/me. It emerged that his cruel wish to intrude on and upset me by threats to exhibit himself carried with it the perverse gratification of believing me to be aroused by such urges—filled, in other words, with his sexual desires and therefore unable to think about his predicament. At the end of this turbulent and distressing session, he brought a memory of having been told that when he was very young in his country of origin, his mother had gone away and he had had to walk in deep snow because his father's back was bad and he was too weak to carry his son. Tom seemed to feel, at this moment, utterly bereft of any parental holding, mental or physical, internal or external. His father (weakened perhaps by Tom's insistent sexual intrusiveness) was felt only to be there when his mother was absent. There was, at this point, no parental couple.

The sessions were now almost too painful to bear. His articulate raving about impending destruction was unstoppable, punctuated only by his howling, gasping, writhing, and sobbing, in an agony of, by turn, terror, rage, and despair. Every experience confirmed his delusory picture of the world and compounded his panic. Like Doris Lessing in *The Golden Notebook,* he felt that he was the only one who could see what was happening to the world. The knowledge and the isolation felt intolerable: the economic system was crushing people to pieces, draining them of any hope or finer feeling. His attacks on his stepfather for similarly crushing and depriving him became ferocious, as did his threats of exposing himself to me, in part as a means of controlling and punishing me for not preventing his deteriorating state. He berated his stepfather for the sadistic negativism shown to him in the past, for his constant belittling and underestimation of Tom, for his imputed glee at Tom's failures, and for his general arrogance and superiority. He blamed his stepfather for his present sense of overwhelming failure.

At the same time, his erotic fantasies about me were scarcely containable. His thinking became increasingly concrete. I misguidedly described him as "stripping" me of my analytic self on one occasion. Tom gasped in recognition. For that was exactly what he was doing—"stripping" me in his mind. So powerful was the externalization of the sexualizing, hating, blaming self, that the "I", in terms of the first-person pronoun, would disappear altogether. Different parts of the self seemed to be at war, with no ego to control or to adjudicate:

> "Feel ill; have to go into College; take library books back; overdue; keep thinking could ring them; fine would be bigger; feel compelled to go in; lecture on stylistics; don't have to do it; must go, must go; unnecessary; got enough war poets; got twenty pages of notes; should be able to do it. Only two thousand words; have to read another book; can't read; have to do four essays; three would do . . . get very distracted."

Tom shouted, groaned, and thumped the couch. He became terrified of putting his feet down on the couch in case, as he acknowledged, he actually messed me up and defiled me with his dirt. In the fantasy of exposing his penis, he wanted to enact his aggressive sexuality and to triumph over me—his mind becoming the capitalist machine grinding me into sexual shape at the expense of my being allowed to be my therapeutic self. Yet there were calmer moments. On one occasion, in response to a noise outside, he moaned that he couldn't bear to have to think that anybody else in the world might have a claim on me. He wept as I spoke of the pain of separation and his jealousy of anyone else in my life. He was briefly in touch with more ordinary, painful oedipal feelings, which hurt him so much. But his state of mind shifted again almost immediately, and he described how talk of loss and separation itself aroused his sexual feelings, "as if I want to be able to hold on to something and keep it".

To deny loss, I suggested, he aroused the fantasy that by keeping me alive sexually he could retain the illusion of keeping control over me. In response he said that the word "porridge" had come to mind—he didn't know why. Puzzled, I waited. After a few moments he recalled a very early memory, before he was 4 years old, he thought. He wouldn't eat his porridge. His mother said that he couldn't have chocolate from the van unless he ate his porridge all up (the arrival of the chocolate-van was a very special event in his life since, at that time, they lived in a remote part of the country, and it came round only once a fortnight). "I shrieked and shrieked, I couldn't believe that she could do that. . . . It seems such a vivid memory, maybe an emotional state more than anything else", he said. I suggested that it felt so cruel of me to give him the nourishing porridge/analysis and deprive him of the sweets that he wanted—the eroticized moments that gave him power to deny separation. "You don't want porridge", I said. He nodded tearfully.

This recognition/acknowledgement of the extent to which he sought, or courted, mental poison (eroticized chocolate), rather than the truth of nourishing mental food, initiated an important shift which had a deep impact on Tom. Despite the pain, he slowly began to turn away from evasion, denial, and sexualization, and towards truthfulness. He had, as in the previous year, requested a letter from the clinic to his college tutor, asking for a deferment of his exams, in mitigation: he was attending the clinic for analysis and was under stress. In the context of wanting a second letter, the issue now posed itself as follows: perhaps it was not so much a question of whether or not the college would believe him, but rather one of whether he could believe himself. Was it really true that he could not sit the exams, or was he trying to enlist the clinic, and me, in a collusive manoeuvre to divert attention from other possible motives for not sitting them with his contemporaries and for being a special case instead? Was he trying to get the clinic, and me, to combine as a parental couple who were prepared to turn a blind eye and become complicit in a lie? If he succeeded in a deferment, he would manage not only to deny his mother the gratification of a graduation day, but also to spite my efforts to support his struggling, thinking self. He wanted both to blame the stepfather/me—"it's all your fault"—and to spite the mother/me, for not giving him what he insisted he most wanted, that is, possession, unchallenged control, and access to what he believed to be the good things.

It became clear that if Tom couldn't achieve a brilliant pass (thereby simultaneously confounding and triumphing over the internal stepfather/me who was felt to have an investment in his failure), he would have to dramatically incapacitate himself (thereby confounding and triumphing over the internal mother/me, who was felt to have an investment in his success). He could thus get the better of me as representing the malign internal couple either by being a success or by being a failure. The latter was a surer bet, rendered more attractive by the fear of losing me should he succeed. For what became increasingly apparent was that an aspect of his panic was lodged in an anxiety that I would mistake prowess in exam-passing for mental health, so that in doing well he would be hastening the end of his analysis. That thought was literally unthinkable: even a whiff of it would stimulate an explosion of anxiety, expressed through sexualized fantasy acting-out elsewhere.

Taking exams represented deep-seated terrors about the nature of his internal relationships, involving blame, hatred, triumph, spite, and denial. Tom was faced with a crisis of unconscious indecision, one in which his thinking capacities became co-opted by a manic and massive externalization of his internal states, which then took over not only the world but also, in fantasy, the mind—my mind, that which had more recently enabled him to hold the boundary between inside and outside reasonably intact. My insistence on the spite and vengefulness that lay behind the apparent incapacity (for which he felt he deserved sympathy and support) was experienced as "running him to ground"—a painful but necessary process leading to a position from which he felt there was no escape. He could then make contact with the possibility of a more benign parental holding which was felt to have his interests genuinely at heart. He began to calm down, to put aside his twenty pages of notes, and to settle for two ordinary, rather than brilliant, essays.

He brought the following dream to the next session (unusually, he had been ten minutes late the previous day):

> *He was supposed to meet a friend, Jack, with whom he was to be doing a painting and decorating job on a house some distance away. Jack had a van and was to drive them to the house. Tom arrived late, anxious, and worried that he was letting down his friend. He then realized that not only was he late, but he had left his tools behind, entailing further delay while Jack drove him home to collect them. Contrary to Tom's fears, Jack was tolerant of the delays and of the extra time needed before they could get on with restoring the house.*

The dream seemed to represent a more accepting and supportive internal figure, one who would be helping Tom to paint and decorate his inner world, who would brook delays and setbacks, and who would help him fetch his thinking capacities and, perhaps, as a combined parental figure (in terms of van and driver), assist in conveying him to the proper site of the work to be done.

There are many possible ways of thinking about this dream: perhaps Jack also represented a friend/father who loans his paternal penis to help decorate/restore the damaged internal mother (or the inside of the internal mother), thus allowing Tom to fetch or to use his own tools/penis for the task. A few weeks later, as his panic lessened still further and his capacity for study increased, a further "house" dream confirmed the changes that I felt were taking place. In this dream the house was no longer in the distance up a cold mountain, but present and available.

He was in a house that was solid, well-built, and rather beautiful. He seemed to be staying there with a group of friends, not his old drinking-companions, but college friends whom he did not yet know very well, but whom he liked a lot and who seemed serious about what they were doing. Among them was a particular woman who had a name similar to mine, Margaret, who had often, in terms of looks, attitude, and qualities, been associated with me. The atmosphere was relaxed. Tom found that he was unusually unstressed, able to talk, to be himself. At one point he was riding a motorbike and stopped to fix an unsafe chain with the help of one of the friends.

This, he interjected, was very different from his early motorbike dreams, and indeed experiences, which had tended to be reckless and often rather out of control. His bikes were constantly in need of repair, and he had a tendency to put his own life, and that of others, at risk. By contrast, he thought that in this dream he felt he had control—"I don't mean in a bad way but I'm somehow able to pursue my own endeavours. It was a good feeling, sort of hopeful. I think maybe I'll come through all this." He then completed his account of the dream:

He spent the night in the house, supposedly alone, his companions seemed to have gone elsewhere. In the morning he discovered that Margaret had also spent the night in the house but without his knowledge. "I wished that I had known, but I also felt very good that she was somehow there with me—she was there, whether I knew it or not."

He acknowledged that the containing-house felt much more solid than those of earlier dreams and that he felt at ease with the figures inside. He had a sense that he was building a stronger relationship with them, but also that they were themselves developing and changing. The motorbike-riding had more the feel of self-expression and individual spontaneity than of self-destruction and gang activity. But perhaps most important and illuminating of all was the description of the Margaret/me figure, somehow there with him, whether he was aware of her or not, present internally as a companion and resource "in the mind". The dream impressed me by the clarity with which it conveyed a particular aspect of the mysterious process of introjection and introjective identification. Having recounted it, Tom said that he wanted to thank me, to express gratitude, make me happy. His saying this immediately put him in mind of his attempts to make his mother happy in the past—both her laughter at his antics but also, and he spoke with sudden, anguished tears, her indifference: when depressed she was unable to respond to him. "My sense of life just drained away", he sobbed. The impact of his despair of ever being able to repair that external mother was very powerful in the room.

This glimpse of a capacity to give and receive happiness seemed inseparable from his mourning for, and resignation to, a damaged external mother whom he could not repair, however deeply, or at times omnipotently, he wished so to do. Perhaps his grief and guilt were more bearable because of a strengthened sense of an internal resource, present irrespective of conscious attention. For Margaret had qualities to which he aspired, and in relation to which he felt humble—ones of integrity, loyalty, helpfulness, friendship, and, perhaps particularly interesting, a firm sense of appropriate boundaries. This sense of aspiration and humility seemed linked to a mode of identification that was now much more introjective than projective.

Tom's struggle to find, and establish, a mind of his own was impressive. The increasing solidity of his internal structure was confirmed, both in his dreams and in his relationships with me and with friends and fellow students. Early on he could hardly have been said to have a mind of his own at all, not one that could be described as carrying any consistent sense of identity. Rather, he had got through life by adopting a series of off-the-peg, look-alike selves of a very two-dimensional kind. The tennis-court area where he had been trying to play out his life had no fourth wall at all and had left him prey to psychotic anxieties and terrors of total emptiness. As his sense of having been walled-up and walled-in all his life increased, and with it the recognition of his need for a protective and containing external and internal space, he began to recognize the existence of the kind of structure that he had so much wanted. It had hitherto seemed very far away and unavailable—the house on the mountain.

His perverse fantasies and activities and his manic omnipotence, though themselves utterly unsatisfying, had functioned as defences against his experiences of loss and abandonment and of the hatred, desolation, and manic triumph that those absences stirred in him. The perversity militated against the capacity to think for himself (or, indeed, often at all), to be small, dependent, to own to his feelings. He found staying on the track of the analysis very difficult, and repeatedly he slipped over the borderline.

Being "run to ground" by me again and again felt like a relief to Tom, despite his resistance to the "porridge". Furious, frustrated, and often desperate that his efforts to seduce me mentally or physically were always doomed to fail, he nonetheless slowly appreciated the protective nature of the various boundaries—of the session times, of the consulting-room, and of my mind itself and its capacity to bear his boundarylessness. Though still wildly jealous, he also, occasionally, felt assured by thoughts of my having a partner and children—having a life, from parts of which he was necessarily excluded. He even felt that, at times, the partnership helped me to help him. By this time we could see that not only did he not have to restore the house all by himself, but that there was a solid house that he could be inside and also a resource present inside himself, whether or not he was always aware of it.

* * *

It would be gratifying to end this chapter on a "happy-ever-after" note, but a characteristic of beginning to establish an identity is that it is beset by all the fiends and demons that lurk in the shadows of potential change, or of progression out of well-tried, albeit painful, anti-developmental modes: the nooks and crannies, in

Tom's case, of dissimulation, perversion, and addiction to mindless states.

It is also a characteristic of working with adolescents that any hopeful notion on the part of the analyst of a "happy-ever-after" state must be resisted. When the established identity is still so fragile, extra stress can at any moment precipitate the emergence—or rather, resurgence—of states of mind that we might wish, or have believed, to belong to the past. To work with this age group is often to work on the borderline: one learns the importance of eschewing notions that we might be "in the clear".

The convergence of a number of factors presented renewed threats to the stability of Tom's sense of being contained internally. As the Easter break from analysis approached, so did his final exams, heralding the end of the structure of the university degree. All this also coincided with having to leave his actual "room" (the house was being sold), as well as the breaking-up of a friendship with a college student which he had hoped might deepen. He had been seeking to care for this young woman, to support and protect her from her own neurotic difficulties, and to rescue himself from the dangers of his eroticization and sexual perversion. The chapter concludes in this more cautionary tone because this encapsulates something of the experience of working with this age group—the difficulty of bearing the fact that there is no certainty, that mental states are in flux, but that nonetheless the carrying of hope is something that the analyst may have to sustain, despite the negative odds.

> Tom dreamt that *he was standing on a station platform waiting for a train that would take him to a station where he was to meet his friend Jack who would help him to move house. Tom felt irritated and worried that Jack would be upset with him for being late. Then suddenly on the far line, a succession, almost a procession, of strange trains drove by—old Underground trains, bizarrely decorated old steam engines, all sorts of extraordinary and exotic locomotives. People on the platform began to clap. Tom joined in, clapping too, as if for a liberating army. Eventually his own train arrived. He later found Jack and Jack's young daughter waiting for him at the designated station. He immediately became struck by the beauty of the*

landscape—not at all as he had remembered it, but cradled in lovely hills, with vague mists, as in a Chinese painting, and, most important of all, in sight of the sea. To his astonishment and perplexity, he found himself in a wonderful seascape. He had remembered a lake in the area but not the sea.

Tom's immediate thought was that the bizarre trains were on the line that was normally the route towards the clinic—the Piccadilly Line, where the direct trains rushed through on the far platform, that is, the one leading towards me. He would, he thought, join one such train further up the line, en route to me. (It is perhaps significant that he had been uncharacteristically late for a number of sessions prior to this dream.)

The dream could be interpreted as describing a state of mind in which a very particular kind of delay occurred, a delay in getting to me, as the Jack/figure of the previous dream, to help him move and settle into a different mind/room. It becomes clear that Tom is still at times too attached to the old trains of thought, bizarre ones (which would seem not to have been entirely superseded by a more direct line). In the dream, these "trains" still command his attention, and he finds himself applauding them. He is worried about being late, but he cannot quite admit that it is those very trains which, far from liberating the warring parts of himself, are in fact delaying his capacity to move on. It looks as though there is a situation in which he delays the process of separation and change, because that process involves the oedipal struggle of working with the reality of me as part of a parental couple, perhaps with a child, standing by to help him. He hangs on to his old trains of thought as a way of putting off this separation. As a consequence, when he does find something good, he idealizes it—"the sea, the sea". That is where the danger lies and will surely do so for some time—in slipping back to a mode of functioning in which the pain of loss is denied in favour of elevating the "special" status of his old ways. This defensive mode holds up the move from the adhesive room to the room of his own. Under the stress of multiple loss, understandably Tom shifts back, perhaps only temporarily, into more familiar, painful, yet gratifying states.

Despite these final words of caution, one cannot but feel hopeful for Tom. Virginia Woolf would have been gratified, but not surprised, that with "a mind of one's own" come renewed creative capacities. Tom began to write—plays and short stories, ones that he felt proud of and were admired by his fellow students and tutors.

Slowly he began to experience the possibility of intimacy and to distinguish between the excitement of his omnipotent, masturbatory experiences on the one hand, and genuine emotion on the other—emotion that put him in touch with his dependency, his littleness, guilt, remorse, and fears of loss. Lacking the sense of an internal parental couple who might have been creatively concerned with his welfare, he had hitherto sought to elide the differentiation between excitement and feeling—attacking and destroying the latter with his perverse states of mind and activities and functioning primarily in Bion's negative grid terms of –L, –H, and –K.

My conjecture was that Tom's developing a mind of his own was based in his increasing dependence on an analyst who was experienced as carrying combined parental functions, with his needs at heart, and able to distinguish his real needs from those based on deception and lies. It was crucial to be able to know the difference between a true struggle towards the capacity for intense and honest links of relatedness and the distortion and perversion of those links, so often lost in a welter of eroticization, grudge-bearing, and pseudo-knowledge. The struggle to sort out the distinction between a genuinely reparative attitude to the various dream rooms and houses, and a papering-over-the-cracks mentality, provided a leitmotif for the analytic work.

Tom's own writing would seem to represent a capacity to begin to set aside lifelong grievances against the tyrannical stepfather, in favour of the introjection of a creative paternal figure linked, surely, to his natural writer-father. Tom's support and concern for the fragilities of a new-found friend also perhaps suggest a burgeoning capacity to care for his damaged internal mother, rather than to berate, blame, or maniacally entertain her.

What Virginia Woolf (1928) tells us she derived from reading *Lear* or *Emma* or *A la Recherche du Temps Perdu* is part of the aesthetic experience that embeds psychoanalysis in the artistic tradition:

> one sees more intensely afterwards; the world seems bared of its coverings and given an intenser life. Those are the enviable people who live at enmity with unreality; and those are the pitiable who are knocked on the head by the thing done without knowing or caring. So that when I ask you to earn money and have a room of your own, I am asking you to live in the presence of reality, an invigorating life, it would appear, whether one can impart it or not. [pp. 108–109]

CHAPTER TWO

Links between internal and external reality in devising a therapeutic setting for adolescents who present with serious conduct disorders

Philippe Jeammet

The increasing number of patients who fall outside the definition of neurosis has, like conduct disorders themselves, led therapists to pay special attention to flaws at a narcissistic level, particularly in the formation of auto-erotism, and to place bonding pathology in a more prominent position than the more classical pathology of conflict. Not that conflicts have vanished: they usually remain the triggering factor and need to be worked through as fully as possible in order to safeguard the future. But for a long time the therapist's chief concern is not so much to help in lifting repression and to find appropriate interpretations as to make such interventions possible without risk for the patient. This involves creating conditions for a therapeutic alliance, and a setting that will enable the process of working through to occur.

We have a twofold aim when working with the adolescents who present to us:

- *To relieve them of debilitating psychiatric symptoms.* Here, their pathology can be seen as loss of freedom of choice, and being locked into repetitious behaviour, which ultimately always means restriction of their human potential. To tackle this, we have various devices in our therapeutic armoury.

- *At the same time, to increase the psychic apparatus's capacity to handle conflict without needing to revert to these symptoms.*

We feel that it is important to keep this twofold aim in mind at every stage of treatment and to organize therapeutic interventions around it. Whatever we do, we must demonstrate that we believe in the adolescent's capacity to take charge of himself. We must show him that we do not think that he has been trapped in his pathology by fate, but that he must give himself a chance to succeed. Of course, development in the patient of the mental capacities necessary to handle conflicts and protect himself is asymptotic, but it is also an unending process, and relapses are a constant danger.

We picture the psychic apparatus as a tool that permits us to handle pleasure and anxiety and enables us to meet our goals. It is located somewhere between the internal world of instinct and need and the world of external reality. It acts as a buffer between the two and therefore carries on the work of the nurturing environment of infancy and childhood—essentially, parental figures. It is a vitally important tool, as it allows us to cope with adversity.

Conduct disorder is a privileged means of expression in adolescence, but is also one of the most difficult problems for a therapist to treat. Better understanding of the psychopathology of behaviour can be helpful in evolving therapeutic responses, which in turn are very much linked to the quality of our relationship with these patients. It is therefore essential to understand what goes on in these relationships (Jeammet, 1994).

We would like to give some examples of the sort of conduct in question. First we will discuss the case of adolescent acting out during spells in institutions such as in-patient services or day-hospitals. These various behaviours have some common features in that they always represent an attack upon the therapeutic setting, and ultimately upon the people who are caring for the adolescents, treating them as things without due regard for their personal wishes and feelings.

When we tried to reconstruct the days and hours that preceded the acts of violence that regularly occur in such institutions, we were surprised to find that the acting out itself was immediately preceded by what the staff called "closeness" or "a moment of closeness". The staff would usually say something like: "We don't understand this act of violence because he was more open than usual yesterday. He started to talk about himself." We hear this again and again: "He seemed happy, he was seen talking to someone." As acting-out behaviour was almost always preceded by this sort of thing, we began to think that it was happening precisely when things were beginning to get better, and especially when there was an opening-up towards others in the psychoanalytic sense, and that this openness upset the self's equilibrium by threatening both intrusion and autonomy, so that the patient reacted by acting out.

We find the same type of features in all adolescent behavioural disorders. Setting aside individual differences and the importance of the choice of behaviour adopted, there are certain shared characteristics amongst acting-out behaviours during adolescence, including eating disorders, drug addiction, suicide attempts, some types of refusal, school apathy, and "active passivity". In all these conducts, the behavioural and motor dimension takes precedence over intra-psychic mental and representational activity.

- It is not unusual to find these different disorders concomitantly or successively in the same person.
- They have become ever more prevalent in the last thirty years in the Western world, and their increase in countries that are gradually becoming Westernized is even more significant. It is this sociological phenomenon that highlights links between individual pathology and sociocultural change, links that probably hinge upon the family unit.
- In the vast majority of cases, it is impossible to subsume these behaviours under any one specific psychiatric heading. They cross the boundaries between diagnostic categories. The difficulties that confront clinicians in this area can be seen in the diverse range of clinical pictures (e.g. anorexia nervosa) or diagnostic categories into which they try to fit behaviours such as suicide or

drug addiction without being able to find any one that addresses the one essential point: the reason why this trouble has appeared now, specifically during adolescence, and why none of the usual symptomatic pictures for particular known psychiatric disorders ever suffice to explain it.

For example, how can reference to hysteria, obsessionality, perversion, or even borderline syndromes help us to understand the appearance of anorexia or suicide attempts? We must obviously take these phenomena into account when setting up a treatment programme and making a prognosis, but they are actually the least representative part of the behavioural problem. Why has the adolescent overstepped the boundaries of these categories? Acting out certainly does lay bare not only the limitations of psychiatric nosography, but also the difficulties—and above all the complexity—of a psychodynamic approach, especially one within an overly strict structural framework. The same observations apply to the way in which these adolescents manage relationships. These are characterized by:

1. alternation between great eagerness for relationships and a tendency to isolate themselves and withdraw, together with intolerance both of loneliness and closeness;
2. keen awareness of the attitude and opinion of other people, often to a hypersensitive degree;
3. difficulty in regulating relationships and in finding an optimal distance, with violent swings between idealized attachment and total severance, vindictiveness, and even outright hostility when faced with the slightest let-down;
4. swings between anxiety due to fear of separation and anxiety due to fear of intrusion;
5. exaggerated expectations of significant others, coexisting with a tendency to be easily influenced, a great capacity for opposition, and an obstinate refusal to change;
6. in much the same vein, extreme sensitivity to the fact that we are interested in them, and that the outcome of treatment depends on the extent to which the therapist believes in the meth-

ods she is using (it is worth noting that any new method will initially have good results in terms of relinquishing symptoms, but that success will lessen as treatment becomes routine; a particular treatment similarly becomes less effective if repeatedly used in relapses);

7. in all cases, self-sabotage, in which the adolescent attacks his own body, or attainments, or inner resources, thereby depriving himself of part of his potential and often what he previously valued most highly.

What, then, is the common denominator, the silver thread, that may link these phenomena and help us to understand the specific way in which puberty sets off these behaviours? The concept of dependency may furnish an answer. A subject whose equilibrium largely depends upon his relationship with external objects and their attitudes can be considered as dependent.

Behavioural disturbance could be seen as a defence against affective dependency if the latter is perceived as a threat to the subject's identity, alienating him from his objects of attachment. In such a system, the subject attempts to substitute bonds of control and ascendancy for affective, relational links that are experienced as all the more threatening precisely because they are so very necessary. The subject's aim is to interpose a behaviour or substitute objects, which he thinks he controls, between himself and his potential attachments: food in bulimia, drugs, food refusal in anorexia nervosa, and so forth.

In such behaviour, we can clearly observe the controlling function of distance in relationships. It allows the subject to maintain apparently satisfying relationships and a relatively diversified social life, but the price he pays is splitting of his ego. Acting-out behaviour and addictive relationships deal with the most conflicted but also the most cathected aspect of relational needs and leave little scope for exchange with other people, which begins to take on a very artificial, predetermined character. Anything reminiscent of an emotional link is rejected. Acting-out behaviour becomes increasingly delibidinalized and purely mechanical, as all fantasy activity attached to it fades away. Auto-erotism loses its erotic, pleasurable aspect. The experience of pleasure is replaced by a need for violent sensation to make the subject feel that he exists. Sensation-seeking then serves to conceal the fear of emotions, in so far as the latter are unavoidable evidence of an object link.

The concept of dependency can lead towards a better understanding of the peculiar dialectical relationship between internal and external reality. If the concept of dependency does not belong, strictly speaking, to classic psychoanalytic terminology, it is nonetheless employed by a great number of psychoanalysts. It is probably used most extensively in Mahler's description (Mahler, Pine, & Bergman, 1975) of the separation/individuation process as a fundamental developmental stage in early childhood. Adolescence, which Blos (1967) regards as the second process of separation/individuation, can be seen as the final stage, or point of collapse, of this struggle for autonomy. Even in France, where psychoanalysts generally consider the approach of Mahler and her successors as too descriptive, in the tradition of Hartmann's autonomous ego, and as departing too far from the current of conflicts, instincts, and sexuality, it still seems difficult to completely abandon the notion of dependency.

André Green, in his paper on *l'archaïque* [the archaic] (1982), also refers to dependency–autonomy as a pair of opposites. His perspective gives meaning to a whole series of behaviours that it would be difficult otherwise to connect. It is all the more interesting in that it links these notions to the concept of the archaic, described in terms of loss of boundaries and of confusion especially between desire, its object, and the ego. Indeed, attacks on limits, unsuccessful differentiation amongst imagoes, and the undifferentiated states to which adolescence is specifically prone all play a key part in bringing the dependency issue to the fore (Jeammet & Chabert, 1998).

Thus, from the point of view of mental functioning, dependency could be described as the defensive use of perceptual-motor reality as countercathexis for a collapsing or dangerous internal psychic reality. Seen this way, dependency becomes a potential or constant feature of mental functioning, since there is always a dialectical interplay of cathexis and countercathexis between internal psychic reality and the external reality of the perceptual-motor world.

From this perspective, we must grant a determining role both to a secure relationship with the environment and to the link between the quality of this relationship and the sort of pleasure that the subject is able to experience through use of his own capacities. Experiences of separation during childhood highlight the quality and reliability of these attainments and enable us to differentiate between children for whom recourse to auto-erotism effectively compensates for the absence of attachment figures, and those who are obliged to replace the latter either by a perceptual-motor cathexis of the environment or else by establishing repetitive self-stimulating activity. Behaviours of the latter sort are all the more massive, mechanical, painful, and even damaging to the subject when links with the environment are weak and the activity bears no relationship with pleasure.

If separation is to be experienced as such, it calls for a distinction to be made between object and subject, similar to the distinction between a symbol and what it symbolizes, but in this case one that presupposes not only a relationship based on difference but also a permanence within the subject of an internal reference that is sufficiently well related to the object without being confused with the object. This is a type of functioning analogous to use of a transitional object, but one that does without the perceptual support furnished by an actual transitional object.

The component auto-erotisms of the narcissistic foundations form the internal reference in question. Auto-erotism consists in an intermittent reinvestment of memory traces of previous satisfactions, something that has become independent of expression of the original need. It is therefore thinkable that the object has left a distinctive mark in the quality of auto-erotic functioning, and that the latter does not involve the erogenous zones alone (mouth, anus, genital organs), even though the fact of their being obligatory points of passage between inside and outside makes them sites of privileged exchanges and tends to focus experiences of pleasure and displeasure upon them. The baby's functioning as a whole—psychomotor as well as physiological—can to a varying extent be seen as having a sort of pleasure grafted on to it, supplied by the nature of the relationship with the cathected object (here, the mother or whoever takes on a mothering role), which in turn confers a particular quality upon the functioning itself. This quality can range through the whole gamut from silent pleasure in functioning to a more or less boisterous erotization.

The infant internalizes this relationship, and it is this internalization that gradually makes him able to wait, or in other words renders him to some extent independent of the actual presence of the external object as a necessary stimulus. It will also form the trace marks or premises of an internal mental representation of the object as such.

Derived from such happy experiences, what goes on inside the baby will secure the foundations of a sense of continuity. In this most basic auto-erotism, one can see a sort of internal framework, a necessary ground, on which the figures of representations of different cathected people will appear and from which they will gradually be detached. Upon this non-conflictual foundation and these internalized experiences, secondary identifications will later develop in ways that are all the more harmonious and narcissistically affirming if these first foundations are securely in place.

In contrast with this harmonious evolution, anything that makes the infant feel the object's weight prematurely, as well as his own helplessness towards it (whether this be due to failings on the object's part or to its excessive presence), is liable to lay the basis for antagonism between the subject and the objects of his cathexes. Narcissistic foundations then no longer get formed with and by the object, steeped in the quality of such a bonded relationship, but against the object.

Where the quality of narcissistic foundations is concerned, another factor has a preponderant influence upon the subject's capacity for autonomy and containment of intra-psychic conflicts: the degree of differentiation amongst the internal structures of the mind. This differentiation seems to go necessarily hand-in-hand with the functionality of the psychic apparatus. The latter cannot fully carry out its role of managing internal pressures and external constraints unless it can, itself, provide an intra-psychic play space that is fit to deal with representational elements (affects and representations) by means of successive displacements that introduce the "little differences" (Freud), so essential for psychic functioning, through which transformational work is carried out that avoids both direct discharge (whether as hallucination or by a perceptual-motor route) and the short circuit of stimulus–response. These differentiated structures correspond with the two Freudian topographies (the conscious, preconscious, and unconscious of the first topography and the id, ego, and superego of the second topography), to which could be added the existence of whole and differentiated parental imagoes and all that has just been said about the makeup of the narcissistic foundations. The existence of such imagoes presupposes that the Oedipus complex has played its part in structuring awareness of the twofold differences between the generations and sexes.

We are using the expression "narcissistic foundations" to describe whatever provides the subject's sense of continuity and enduring cathexis of himself. They rest upon various underlying supports, all of which have in common a dialectical opposition with whatever remains available for object cathexis. However, this particular dialectical opposition is founded on a double paradox, since narcissistic foundations can only be built on the basis of object relations (though in such a way that opposition between subject and object is not even an issue), while the more that solidly narcissistic foundations are established, the less will "object-seeking" be experienced as "anti-narcissistic".

What changes, then, might upset this balance in the interplay of cathexis and countercathexis? Ones that lend extra weight to objects and accentuate the attraction they exert. Some types of cathexis are clearly less tolerable than others, and this is the case with cathexes of objects whose relationship with the subject, often unconsciously, is one of expectation and authority. Sexualization of this type of relationship plays a powerful part in the arousal of dependency fears and occurs both in relationships that have or acquire an incestuous dimension and in ones that evoke fantasies of passive receptivity. Arousal of homosexual desire combines all these factors both in its narcissistic and in its sexual dimensions. In the sexual dimension, fantasies of anal penetration are a particularly active source of intrusion anxiety.

Relationships that spark off identification processes have the particularity of combining all these factors, as happens in adolescence. There are also relationships that thwart the defences mentioned above—for instance, if there is a brutal dis-idealization or sexualization of a relationship that had remained safe until then. In fact, we have in mind any source of imbalance in object relations that is liable to give rise to phenomena of envy by assigning more power to the objects in question. This shift can be caused by an object itself or by something in the subject's internal world—for instance, the sudden pressure of identificatory longing.

Adolescence brings all these factors together. Its effect is to reveal internalization difficulties from early childhood and any dependency issues that had so far remained latent. The effects of potential dependency, of sexualization of the adolescent's body and relationships, and of renewed oedipal conflict, all unite to potentialize the traumatic effects of each factor taken separately, mutually reinforcing one another. The distinctive, delayed effect of puberty seems therefore to be twofold: revelation of the genital sexual nature of childhood events and fantasies, and revelation of unresolved dependency situations from childhood, together with the power that the latter confer upon objects whose "influence on him" the adolescent suddenly recognizes, along with the narcissistic threat that such objects pose. This dual effect could well account for the traumatic potential of puberty in some personalities. Dependency on external objects can give incestuous fantasy the undeniable stamp of reality, and the twin problems of dependency and sexualization then compound their effects upon identification. It becomes impossible to finalize identification processes, which are robbed of their symbolic momentum by the concretization of fantasy. Identifying with someone means not becoming like the other person but actually taking his place. Incestuous and parricidal fantasies thereby take on a reality that makes even thinking about them dangerous (Sprince, 1988).

The threat to narcissistic autonomy represented by the awakening of object need can easily spread to need itself—that is, to its instinctual source. Need is no longer perceived as the emergence of the subject's own desire and a potential enrichment for the ego, but as a threat. The subject then feels dependent on the object of satisfaction, which causes him to treat desires and instincts as external objects and to apply the same defensive measures to them.

Many adolescents face what we see as a truly paradoxical situation when their affective dependency puts them in direct contradiction with a need to assert their autonomy. The paradox could be expressed in the following terms: "What I need is a threat to my autonomy precisely because I need it. The more the need is felt, the greater the threat." This situation leads them to refuse their own need and aggravate their dependency by stopping the process of internalization that is necessary if the identification process is to be accomplished. This process tends to be self-perpetuating and to worsen, creating a vicious cycle.

We find that this situation, in which the adolescent feels his very identity threatened by his relational needs, produces defensive reactions in the form of acting out and behavioural disturbance. All adolescent conduct pathology seems to include this dimension, which must therefore be taken into account when devising therapeutic measures. Indeed, the more necessary relationships actually are for these adolescents, the more intolerable they appear to be. Conduct disorders can then be seen as playing a role in the internal equilibrium of the adolescent, regulating distance in his relationships with others.

Violence, for instance, seems to allow the self to pull together when threatened by loss of identity or loss of boundaries. Even the most brutal acting out does not happen by chance. Violence always serves a purpose in the psychic economy, and in my view it is essential in protecting the self. It releases the self's internal tensions, which threaten to overflow, while at the same time allowing control of the object by supplanting it and freeing the self of its influence.

Every act of violence reinforces the boundaries between self and object. Physical blows are a good example. When you strike someone, not only do you touch him, but you differentiate yourself from him and oppose him. A blow creates contact while simultaneously denying one's need for contact.

We can see how adolescents may assuage their depersonalization crisis by means of masochistic acts like burning themselves with a cigarette, and how this act helps them to find themselves again. Pleasure, especially sexual pleasure, can provoke depersonalization because one loses one's sense of boundaries. By contrast, pain—provided that it does not go too far—can re-establish a sense of boundaries and, by this means, help the subject find himself again.

We could compare the self's pulling together in this way to a nightmare from which one wakes and says, "Wait—it was only a dream". One usually wakes at precisely the moment when the object is catching up with one or when one can no longer escape the situation. The object and the situation represent something that is desired, but from which one also wants to flee. This "invasion" threatens the self's capacity to work on the experience and maintain control. Waking up from a nightmare is a form of acting out. It is like getting up and running away from a psychotherapeutic situation that is too difficult to handle. The sleeper awakes, and the conscious self puts everything outside itself: "That's not me, or mine. It has nothing to do with me." By waking up, the subject countercathects his internal world by over-investing the perceptual world of external reality.

The threat that the awakening of object needs poses for narcissistic autonomy may be extended to need itself, and therefore to instinct. Instinct is no longer felt to be a potential means of enrichment for the self but, rather, as a threat that makes the self dependent upon an object. The self will then be obliged to deal with desire and impulses as though they were external objects and to apply defensive strategies to them.

We can see how ambiguous and unsatisfactory this doubly protective function of deviant behaviour actually is. At first, it does indeed protect the most important object relationships by deterring any potential for conflict with the subject. It offers protection at the narcissistic level by attributing anti-object and self-management functions to the behaviour.

However, in the long run deviant behaviour reverses its role of object and narcissistic protector and becomes just the opposite. To this must be added the fact that the fear of potential object dependency is replaced by very real dependency on the behaviour.

All this means that the adolescent may find himself deprived of what he needs most in order to achieve identification: the indispensable support of object relationships, especially in their sexual dimension, which is all the more important now because his previous internalizations have partially failed. The adolescent will then have to use distancing mechanisms with the very objects he most highly valued, eliminating tender relationships that might otherwise have both helped him to handle necessary introjections, especially homosexual ones, and reinforced his narcissism.

Instead, reversal into opposites and reversal against the self will appear and give way to masochistic and self-sabotaging behaviour. This may at first preserve object relations but later on will increase dependency and object intolerance.

These self-sabotaging behaviours that indicate dependency and reveal the partial failure of internal psychic processes have several economic functions:

- they give rise to a neo-language between the adolescent and his family, becoming increasingly important and gradually cutting off other forms of interchange;
- they act as a mediator between the adolescent and his valued objects;
- they become his "thing", his creation, that which he cherishes above all else, and in the end they take the shape of a neo-identity which he has constructed entirely on his own, thereby denying any role to his parents and the primal scene.

These behaviours also have a tendency to be self-reinforcing, and the adolescent engages in the same sort of dependency toward them as he was trying to avoid with his objects. They are serious because, in contrast with object relations, they offer no support for his narcissism. The benefit afforded by the sense of control they confer can only be experienced as long as the behaviour continues, and meanwhile actual need for objects and for internal emptiness inexorably grows.

A good example of this is the frequent reinforcement of such behaviours (anorexia, bulimia, suicide attempts) during psychotherapy. It is not unusual to see a marked contrast between a therapist's satisfaction based on material expressed and worked through by the patient and a worsening of symptomatic behaviour. This does not mean that the therapy is not working: on the contrary, the patient can only find one way to control a transference investment that is too overwhelming—namely, to increase his deviant behaviour.

We can therefore see that the behaviour serves to protect him from his object, which may lead the adolescent to step up his deviant behaviour and wipe out all traces of attachment to the object. The behaviour itself loses all libidinal potential and becomes increasingly mechanical. Fantasies connected with the behaviour gradually disappear. Auto-erotic activities lose their eroticism and pleasure. Violent sensations become a vital necessity and no longer merely a route to pleasure. These behaviours not only deprive the adolescent of his narcissism and reinforce his fear of dependency, they also become a drug. They serve as an important defence against castration and separation anxiety as well as against depression.

Negative conduct aggravates the adolescent's narcissistic depletion while reinforcing his fear of being dependent upon the objects of his desire. It also creates a sort of addictive fascination. For a long time it provides a strong defence against anxiety as well as depression. Having success and pleasure makes one dependent upon the person who confers those feelings. One is reliant on what that person thinks, but success is short-lived. One is constantly obliged to try again, with uncertainty about the outcome. There is always a risk of disappointment.

With negative behaviour, implying as it does a refusal to fail, the subject is always the one who controls the situation: no more submission to the whims of other people's opinions, no more fear of loss or separation. Instead, there is a feeling of control of the situation. There is, however, a price to pay—the sacrifice of pleasure—although the adolescent may continue secretly to think that if he wanted to, he could return things to the way they were before. This idea represents a more or less conscious fantasy that his possessive bond with his archaic objects is permanent.

This self-perpetuating and self-reinforcing process relentlessly indicates the transfer of the dependency issue onto relationships. Under these circumstances, desire is perceived as an expression of dependency on the desired object, who tends to become confused with the source of instinctual drive. The object thus acquires anti-narcissistic significance instead of being a means of strengthening the self by using identification mechanisms. Everything that increases the object's appeal and makes it exciting also turns it into a threat to the self's integrity and boundaries. Likewise, everything that helps to erase the boundaries between self and object makes the object seem too exciting. Bonds of an incestuous nature have both these characteristics, which makes them especially threatening.

Therapeutic implications

This view of acting-out behaviours as attempts at regulating relationships with external objects who have been imbued with functions of establishing internal psychic equilibrium and countercathexis of internal objects, has concrete implications for our approach and therapeutic attitude towards these patients. The difficulty resides essentially in the need to solicit object-seeking that is bearable without resort to acting-out behaviours.

Both the quality of his narcissistic foundations and the degree to which his psychic apparatus and its agencies are differentiated contribute to the adolescent's security and safeguard him from the risks entailed by transference. But this differentiation is often damaged during adolescence precisely by regressive activity.

The need to cling to external reality makes the latter all the more arousing. It is therefore important to organize a setting in external reality that is capable of bearing the differentiating functions that are threatened by the adolescent process itself.

In this context, one can see how the therapist has a potentially traumatic part to play. Simply and solely because he offers himself as an object for investment, he presents the menace of a seductiveness that may be felt as a violently intrusive threat to the adolescent's narcissism and will generate antagonism between object-need and the threat it poses to his narcissism and autonomy. We therefore think that reactivation of homosexual feeling, connected with the reverse side of the Oedipus complex, may be the point around which this antagonism tends to crystallize. This in fact connects both with narcissistic problems of reference and with object-related issues to do with the identificatory process.

Although largely unconscious, these matters are active in the interplay between the internal world of representations and the external world of percepts. The latter is at once a receptacle for countercathexes of anxiety-laden unconscious or preconscious representations and an indirect means of giving them shape. For this reason, the therapist's perceived reality is no indifferent matter—this goes, above all, for the therapist's gender, but also for her (or his) age and appearance in general, together with whatever resonances these factors have for the adolescent. This often influences the establishment of the transference and how stimulating it is—in other words, the degree to which it is bearable.

The therapist is therefore placed from the start in a potentially seductive position. The excitement she awakens may provoke a sort of delayed-action effect wherein infantile expectations and traumas are sexualized. This accounts for the difficulty in managing a therapeutic relationship with adolescents and the danger of getting drawn into a totalitarian relationship in which the enormity of the unconscious investment has a detrimental effect upon its differentiated status. I also wonder whether the setting itself is not responsible for part of the adolescent's response. In other words, if an adolescent is thrown into an overly close or overstimulating relationship, one is going to find undifferentiated activity and massive investment.

This difficulty in managing the transference tends to recur in problems with interpreting to adolescents. The specificity of interpretation is bound up with the specificity of transference phenomena at this age and the fact that both imply reference to infantile matters.

Interpretation links three persons: the patient, the therapist, and the infantile imago. This is what defines interpretation, and it is precisely the fact that it concerns these three levels that it needs to be managed in a particular way during adolescence, due to the peculiar nature of the bonds that link a patient of this age to his infantile objects, his childhood, and his parents, as well as to the therapist through the transference.

It is not obvious how to manage this triangulation during adolescence, since interpretation explicitly refers to something absent—the infantile object—which is very much present in the patient's head but does not appear amongst his external, perceptual, sources of support, notably his father or mother. Going beyond the relationship with the therapist to implicate someone absent leads in particular to problems with separation and therefore also to dangers of destruction and loss. The risk is therefore twofold—of an overly sudden renewal of problems to do with absence, and of going back to babyhood.

Reference to infancy can be anxiety-provoking in so far as it reactivates ties with childhood, something from which the adolescent is trying to detach himself, and it also confronts him with a certain tendency to be passive connected with his infantile experience. These two parameters—reference to someone absent from perceptual reality and a return to infantile experience—coincide in loss of control.

Loss of perceptual control redoubles the effect of the passivity connected with returning to infancy in interpretations and can pose a threat to the adolescent's narcissistic equilibrium.

Returning to infancy also raises the question of regression and its toleration, especially by adolescents. We therefore face a real dilemma. Is an adolescent capable of going through this regression without undue risk? Is it as necessary for an adolescent as it would be for an adult undergoing classical treatment?

Most of the time the answer is no; conduct disorders and acting out are already forms of regression. They repeat infantile situations but occur without remembrance (Freud, 1914g). We must not, therefore, encourage regression that has already broken through the ego's capacity for containment. Rather, we must strengthen its capacity to forge links and recollect. This can be achieved in several ways:

- by reactivating positive auto-erotisms and a pleasure in working well (especially in psychotherapeutic exchanges and, if necessary, in institutional care), which strengthen narcissistic foundations;
- by reinforcing the ego's essential means of differentiation by using the representational support that external, perceptual reality affords (for instance, the therapist's reality; enlisting an actual third party through use of bi-focal therapies, as discussed below, or resorting to institutions; or protecting it from threats of undifferentiation and engulfment connected with the transference);
- by easing the weight of destructive fantasy by means of clarification and naming feelings and expectations connected with the present state of the cathected relationship with the therapist.

The question of lateral transference arises as a transference relationship develops in this way. This is a situation often encountered in adolescence, and one must be careful not to interpret it too quickly or to regard it only as a defensive manoeuvre likely to deprive therapy of an essential investment. In fact, it often helps to make transference to the therapist bearable by keeping its existence partially out of awareness, while allowing feelings to be talked about that would be impossible if the adolescent had to address them directly with the therapist. It is not the depth of repression that prevents their expression but rather its insufficiency that makes the adolescent permanently afraid of being overwhelmed by the intensity and crudity of his emotions. The free play of repression and displacement that cannot take place intrapsychically is replaced by use of external representational props; for example, when faced with the intensity of transference investment in his therapist, the adolescent may take back part of his investment by using lateral transference. The initial investment always concerns the same internal object and is exempt from any intrapsychic work of modification or displacement. Instead, by distributing its investment like this amongst various different external supports the ego protects itself from the risk of being overwhelmed. Unawareness of the univocal nature of the investment takes the place of repression and permits the adolescent a certain freedom of expression of feelings that assists the ego in its effort to integrate.

The practice of psychoanalytic psychodrama has promoted familiarity with this use of external reality and the perceptual-motor world, notably because therapeutic players act as perceptible props for aspects of intrapsychic reality that escape preconscious representational work because of the enormity of the affects that foster processes of de-differentiation at the expense of any effort to represent them.

To achieve its ends, psychodrama makes deliberate use of one of the patients' most active and massive defence mechanisms—projection into the external world of their own interiority. It is therefore from the outside, by means of what a particular patient has offered from his inner world, and in his own words, that an attempt is made to get him to re-internalize his "internal theatre", once he has become aware of it and has had a chance to play around with its multiple cast. This means offering the patient use of techniques like repeated scenes, voice-off commentary, doubling, and being a spectator.

Recourse to the perceptual world cannot therefore only be viewed in terms of evacuation of whatever the ego cannot bear, but also more positively as a means by which the ego can preserve its functioning by finding external support where it is lacking internally. "The mind is the space in which the representable can occur" (Green, 1995). But representation goes on at several different levels. The ego can use external figurative props, as well as counter-investment of internal reality by resorting to the perceptual world, to bolster its efforts to represent at times when it is faced with primary forms of representation. These may consist, for example, of unconscious, condensed, and poorly differentiated representations that are barely accessible to the self except in the form of massive affects that do more to inhibit than stimulate thought and the potential for displacement. In this situation, external, figurative reality can play an economic role by mobilizing a differential third party. It enables us to speak in terms of the emergence of mind, and of correspondence between an external psychic space and an internal psychic space.

From an analytic viewpoint, this kind of externalized representation of fantasies that patients express, which we often even anticipate by lending help, offers, together with psychodrama, an important alternative method because it indicates a way ahead in the opposite direction to the one constantly taken in classical treatment. Nonetheless, this diversity of means has a single end, which is one of confronting the subject with fantasy productions whose authorship he might recognize as his own. It is, in effect, a condition sine qua non for interpretations to make sense and eventually acquire "mutative value".

What changes, therefore, is the way in which the basic tools of the psychoanalytic method are used. In psychodrama, they are used specifically to reinforce support of patients' mental processes by means of the setting. This depends essentially upon two different things that are mutually supportive and complementary: help with figuration processes and thereby also with linking, and strengthening factors that promote differentiation.

Help with figuration processes is a direct consequence of setting up a psychodramatic framework and applies at every step of psychodrama: help by the play's leader with expression and formalization of the scenes proposed by the patient; intervention in the play by co-therapists, who, as noted above, may choose to do this in a multitude of different ways which thereby allow all of the mind's modes of expression to be represented: unconscious or preconscious fantasies, instinctual drives, psychic agencies, and so forth; and interruption of the scene by the play's leader, followed in due course by interpretative work or simply explanation and commentary.

Pleasure in actually playing is a powerful factor in achieving figuration and connecting feelings, as is the concreteness afforded by the scene being played and the physical contact during it. As Chabert (1997) reminds us, experiences at a bodily level are specifically solicited by psychodrama. They take on meaning in the subject's history through the recollection process, and also in the present reality of the transference relationship, as they are talked about or simply shared in exchanges during the play. The presence of the play's leader and co-therapists allows for explicit recognition of this, which thereby incorporates the experience into an object relationship while at the same time making it more bearable and less guilt-ridden. This is especially so because watching by the group plays the role of a superego third party.

Psychodrama sustains and strengthens factors that promote differentiation. It does this partly by means of processes of figuration and decondensation that have already been described, and also through the immediate support by the perceptual-motor world that it offers the patient and is provided by the psychodrama setting properly so called. In this respect, it runs counter to classical treatment and has more in common with face-to-face psychotherapy. It goes even further than the latter by multiplying the number of therapists and giving scope for motor activity. At its limits, it can even supply words on the patient's behalf, at least for a time, because when co-therapists express themselves it is always partially in the patient's stead, and there may be a total replacement when they act as his double When a patient is blocked, the therapist sometimes proposes playing a scene for him.

Boundaries are constantly being preserved by this recourse to external reality—boundaries between self and other, and between internal and external worlds—while at the same time the psychodramatic play space lends support to virtual, intrapsychic space and the imaginary boundaries amongst the intra-psychic agencies.

From this it follows that psychodramatic play is an analogical representation of intra-psychic space and its imaginary contents: paternal and maternal imagoes, superego, id, and ego, and their various component parts are given concrete support by different contributors. Everything, even ambivalent feelings, can be materialized by one actor or another in the play, while the patient—whose very tendency to condense and de-differentiate makes cathexis dangerous for his narcissistic autonomy—is potentially protected from the enormity of the transference by its dilution across a number of participants and its mediation by third parties present.

We have developed a point of view (Kestemberg & Jeammet, 1987) from the perspective of which psychodrama could be regarded as an auxiliary aid to mental functioning as a whole because of the potential it offers for externalizing psychic functions and supporting their figuration and differentiation. Here we might mention simply its salient features: it gets the work of figuration going again, it provides conditions for displacing and linking affects and representations, it employs negation and object splitting, and it revives an interplay between introjection and projection. Indeed, psychodrama constantly solicits negation, a mechanism that Freud accorded an essential place in strengthening the ego and enriching psychic life. It makes maintenance of repression less necessary by allowing representations to gain access to the ego while still holding affects at a distance. Conversely, where repression has been inadequate, it helps to free the ego from affective overload while at the same time making it possible to work on the content of representations that are too exciting to be completely accepted and assimilated. Here, play by co-therapists offers the patient the opportunity par excellence to grasp the content of such representations while only recognizing as his or her own those aspects of them that the patient can in fact tolerate.

A whole range of representations is therefore offered to the patient, enriching his potential for representation but without imposing them upon him as coming from himself and "betraying" him. This is all the more effective because the "injection of fantasies" by the players, and the offer of representations more generally, is proposed by the co-therapists and not by the play leader, who bears the strictest, if not the most intense, cathexis because of his role as superego or ego ideal. Playing allows for a juxtaposition of opposites that the patient is not obliged to take back immediately and completely to his own account; it also allows for object splitting that can highlight but also mitigate splits in the ego on which it can then become possible to work without attacking the patient's ego.

The whole set-up of a psychodrama is designed to support work that the patient's preconscious cannot perform on its own and which the transference solicitation of classical psychotherapy runs a greater risk of hindering than of helping. It involves reconciling opposites: facilitating the emergence of fantasy and re-actualizing buried memories and bodily sensations while at the same time limiting regression and promoting symbolization. The fiction of play and the direct involvement of co-therapists make possible the first two requirements without inducing a serious regression in the patient's ego, while the division of roles (patient, leader, co-therapists) and also the fictionality of the play and the primacy accorded to verbalization sustain the process of symbolization. Psychodramatic play is not an inducement to act out, but seeks alliance, instead, with the truth of experience and with the distancing afforded by contrast between the current and the historical and between expression in action and in words. Two technical points seem fundamental both to this inducement to symbolize and to management of the patient's response: the suspension of action implied by the "as-if" of the play, and the symbolic strength of non-participation on the part of the play leader, which valorizes the two means of communication that he does possess—looking and speaking—whose genetic links with superego function are well known, as are the superego's links with symbolization.

The therapeutic process cannot now focus on internal reality alone, in terms of which use of external reality might otherwise be interpreted. It proceeds, instead, by managing the latter in such a way as to strengthen the ego's capacity for working through and, secondarily, by allowing gradual recognition of the patient's internal reality, which goes hand in hand with reconstruction of an internal space composed of representations that have once more become accessible to secondary processes. After this detour through perceptual reality, and its therapeutic management in a manner analogous with maternal reverie which, in Bion's view, transforms beta elements into alpha elements, there comes a time when an internal psychic space, now restored to working order, is reinvested. Above all, it is the renewal of libidinal ties, now rendered bearable—in other words, the effort to re-objectalize—that permits internalization to take place, notably by authorizing reactivation of auto-erotisms whose pleasurable quality is due to the quality of the object relations that underlie them. Brusset (1990) illustrated this process very explicitly in connection with the transformation during treatment of addictive wanderings on the part of an anorexic girl into the sort of auto-erotic activity I have just described.

Example

The history of Marie, a 14-year-old anorexic girl, illustrates one such necessary detour through a management of external reality designed to mobilize a frozen internal psychic reality. Her anorexia nervosa had begun before puberty at 11 years of age, a form which is known to be especially severe. It is often life-threatening, seriously inhibits growth, and goes hand in hand with grave distortions of personality. This form of anorexia contrasts with those that accompany the first physical signs of puberty and are often reactive to puberty in character and have a better prognosis.

Marie's anorexia was of the severe type. She was disturbingly underweight (25 kg). Her growth had stopped at a height of 140 cm. She was in total denial of her thinness and of having any personal difficulties, and she was as implacably opposed to a psychotherapeutic relationship as she was to food. The onset of her anorexia at 11 years of age had coincided with an episode of depression and withdrawal in her mother, who was preoccupied with grief at her own mother's death, while Marie's sister, three years older than herself, escaped into adolescence. This "abandonment" by mother and sister seems to have re-actualized for Marie the "trauma" of the birth of a baby brother when she was four years old; she had also known that her parents had hoped for a boy when she herself had been born. As a small child, Marie seems to have massively countercathected her death wishes and ambivalence towards her little brother and her mother through numerous reaction-formations and a dependent and controlling relationship with her mother.

Marie's anorexia refocused her parents' interest on her, got her mother partially out of her depression, and strengthened their reciprocal ties of dependency, while her father made strenuous efforts to cure her by taking her feeding in hand and by giving in to all her demands to buy clothes and a large Mickey Mouse collection from repeated visits to Disneyland. But these apparent secondary benefits were offset by an aggravation in her state that threatened her life, and she inevitably needed hospital treatment. She was hospitalized several times, but each discharge led rapidly to a disturbing loss of weight. In the space of three years she had spent twenty months in hospital.

It was during her last spell in hospital that psychodrama was set up. This was a particularly difficult period because, apart from the physical danger, it was accompanied by long series of daily escapes when she would run away to join her family, who regularly brought her back on the strength of the therapeutic alliance forged with them and the gravity of the breakdown of previous attempts to leave hospital. Faced with refusal of any sort of psychotherapy, the meagre results of regular family meetings, and the violence of her behaviour, the therapeutic team began to feel that it had reached an impasse. This apparent refusal of care contrasted, however, with a massive investment in the service and its caregivers which was evident in Marie's day-to-day life despite her negations and repeated escapes. As for many of these patients, but in a particularly acute way, cathexis of therapeutic staff seemed to pose a twofold threat to Marie: of being engulfed by her own investment in them, and of destroying links with her family in a manner that was perfectly analogous to the terror that her repressed bulimic yearnings inspired in her. Faced with this impasse, we decided, as always in such cases, to try to open things up, this time by using individual psychoanalytic psychodrama. This was imposed rather than suggested, since the patient was refusing; Marie in fact only conceded under the concerted pressure of her parents and the doctor in charge of her case at the hospital unit.

The psychodrama was to be directed by me. She knew that I was the head of the service, and she was used to seeing me at the staff–patient meetings that I run at the hospital unit twice every month. I was also known to her parents through the meetings for parents of anorexic patients that I organize every three weeks. This decision represented an important narcissistic gratification for Marie in so far as I am not directly involved with hospitalized patients. We have now had two years of psychodrama, eight months of which were while she was still in hospital, on the basis of one 30-minute session per week, while she has also continued to attend meetings with staff at the hospital unit and the family meetings.

The running away stopped as soon as psychodrama began, even though Marie demonstrated noisily—and sometimes grossly—her refusal to cooperate in psychodrama, which she considered "stupid". Her refusal to suggest scenes led me as director of the play to do so in her place. She would then play, but stuck wilfully to realism, refusing to take any role other than her own and distancing herself from any suggestion that might take her away from what she saw as the "reality" of what might have been said or done if a given scene had been "for real". She would stop in its tracks every imaginary digression risked by one of the co-therapist players. She mostly refused to select co-therapists to be partners in a scene, and I was obliged to nominate one or more in her stead.

As her co-therapists continued, despite everything, to say things that she considered "unacceptable" because she deemed them purely "imaginary", she finally refused to play at all. It was then decided to play without her, a most unusual situation, with myself proposing the subject of the scene and choosing the players, including one to play her part. Paradoxically, this atypical situation gave us more freedom, and it was possible for the co-therapist who played her role to give free scope to the expression of rather crude fantasies, notably concerning rivalry with her brother and death wishes towards him as well as towards her mother. We also played her oedipal disappointment with her father, who was guilty of betraying her by making a little brother to replace the boy that she herself was not. She often accused us, with great vehemence, of wanting to drive her mad by ascribing thoughts to her that she did not have. To this the play leader, in commentaries that followed the scenes, would reply that this was only what we imagined a little girl might feel and think in a situation like her own at that time, but that we were not inside her head and were perhaps mistaken, and in any case she was not obliged to agree: she could always intervene herself in the scene to correct it. She did do this with increasing frequency, giving her version and above all making statements about what she was thinking in the present, usually refusing to make even the slightest reference to the past. This period saw an intensification of obsessional rituals that had appeared during her hospitalization and which consisted essentially in taking one step back after several steps forward in a manner that was extremely restrictive and even incapacitating. At the same time, she gained weight gradually without any need to resort to tube-feeding. She would protest during the play but, contrary to our expectations, would listen, sometimes ostentatiously turning her back; above all, she started coming spontaneously to psychodrama without needing to be escorted by a nurse, as had been the case in the beginning.

Marie then began gradually to play and even to propose scenes. She never explicitly took on as her own the destructive fantasies, but she did for the first time give evidence of tender feelings towards her little brother, accompanied in reality by a new complicity with him. At this point she brought her first dream. It was a nightmare: "*She had put on 4.8 kg.*" She violently refused to play the dream. I proposed that someone should play in her place a scene in which the birth of the little brother was being announced. Marie and her father, mother, and big sister were gathered together, and the mother was being congratulated on the birth of this baby "weighing over 4 kg", while his sister was amazed by the disappearance of her mother's big tummy and was wondering whether a baby was like pooh that you get rid of when you go to the toilet. Marie offered no commentary but was flustered and lost track of who was playing her own part in the scene. After a scene that took up previous proposals of hers expressing horror at the possibility of having a "little round tummy", a co-therapist playing her double expressed her wish to destroy the baby inside her mother's tummy and a wish to empty it of its contents. Marie then became able to talk about her fascination as a little girl with her mother's "round tummy", recalling having stroked it. In the commentary that followed the scene, it was possible to call to mind her wish that when she became a young woman like her sister, she might have a round tummy with a baby inside like her mother. She said nothing to challenge this, but in the following weeks began to go out with this sister and her boyfriend, then with a girlfriend of her own, while at the same time she became more feminine in her physical appearance and swapped her jeans and collections of Walt Disney objects for more feminine clothing. At the same time, she made an object split amongst her therapists. She rejected and refused to play with one of the male co-therapists who was of the same origin as her father and whom she had regularly chosen in the past to act her father's part. In her view, he was guilty of having alluded to her physical figure during one scene. But at the same time she drew noticeably closer to me, even apologizing for proposals she had made at the beginning of psychodrama that were hurtful to me and acknowledging that she liked me a lot. In parallel, relations with her parents relaxed. Her weight began to approach the normal, and she accepted leaving the hospital service for a medico-pedagogic boarding-school, where she resumed her studies while continuing to come once a week for psychodrama. She made friends with a girl at the boarding-school who was also anorexic. She found her "really too thin" and tried to help her understand what was going on inside her and to start eating again.

Today, Marie presents as a pleasant, attractive young woman of normal weight and able to take care of herself. She has resumed satisfactory study at an ordinary mainstream school and has returned home to her parents. Her pubertal develop-

> ment has recommenced. She is not yet menstruating, but her breasts have formed and she has grown several centimetres. She remains vulnerable, however, and one senses that her narcissistic balance still remains broadly dependent upon how she is regarded. If wounded too greatly, she could turn in upon herself again and lock herself into a negativist attitude, even if it did not necessarily take the form of an anorexia. She remains anxious and dreads everything that she cannot control. She comes back to see me regularly, about once a month, to "take stock" of her development. In my own mind this serves above all to maintain her narcissistic support by assuring her implicitly of my interest in her. She says that she is rather anxious about "her shape", but now she means not the shape of her body in general but very specifically the shape of her breasts. She has decided for herself to go back to see a psychotherapist, a woman, whom she knew at the beginning of her anorexia, before hospitalization and psychodrama, but whom she had previously refused to contact.

This observation illustrates the defiance one is up against in a psychoanalytic approach to these cases. In the first place, there are ambiguities in demand. Marie expected people to care for her, but it was the very intensity of her expectation that made it unbearable. The more a demand engages a subject's narcissism, the less the ego can bear it, something that is illustrated by perfect analogy in the coupling of anorexia and bulimia. Narcissism is likely to be engaged most extensively if what we have defined as narcissistic foundations are insecurely established. They in turn will be challenged most strongly if cathected objects are too exciting, either because of libidinal ties—particularly ones of an incestuous nature—or because of aggression and destructive threats towards such ties. Aggression and sexual excitement are also liable to be mutually reinforcing, as perversions illustrate, but so too is the "perverse setup" of behavioural disorders once they are organized (Jeammet, 1994). Destructive threats to internal objects only intensify the need to cling defensively to external objects. Such interlocking between narcissistic and object relationships is characteristic of the behaviour pathology in question, which is also of necessity a boundary pathology. Cathexis of an object then represents a threat both to narcissism and identity. The degree of narcissistic engagement is highlighted by the extent of mirroring phenomena and reversal into opposites. The subject who is acting out treats his object as he himself feels treated and makes it suffer what he constantly dreads suffering, something that the transference relationship brings out. Adolescence particularly aggravates this set of problems.

The psychic internal world, and especially affects in so far as they are linked with objects, is then treated as an external object threatening the ego. Emotions are like the object's Trojan Horse inside the ego. Denial and projection, and reversal into opposites, are the preferred defence mechanisms. Turning in against the self, which can lead into the whole area of masochism, is one way to preserve a bond with an object.

A therapeutic approach must use the same channels as the ego's defences, but in reverse. Representations that the ego refuses will be offered for figuration through a perceptual route. This offers a prospect of mastery through visual control and guarantees the exteriority that is reassuring to the ego.

This was going on when Marie began to recognize and talk about the dangers of anorexia in connection with her friend at boarding-school. It was also happening earlier on when she gradually moved towards figuration of possible feelings and then their recognition and partial re-appropriation through play by co-therapists. She thereby passed from denial of her internal world to its negation. This is a fundamental process, as Freud emphasized in his paper on negation (1925h), because it represents an important step in the lifting of repression (or reduction of denial) in that it allows access to conscious representation of the repressed while at the same time refusing ownership of it by attributing it elsewhere.

A space for play develops in the external scene instead of, and in the place of, the inaccessible internal psychic space. Play then begins in the manner of the cotton-reel game (*fort–da*) described by Freud (1920g) in connection with his grandson and moves on to play within Winnicott's transitional space (1971). Repetition is an attempt at magical mastery of separation. For Marie, it reassured her that she could stay in a two-dimensional world, with her conscious thoughts on one side and perceptual reality on the other. She was very willing to play with us at times, but only to reiterate, "this is stupid—it isn't even true", as small children may do when hearing an anxiety-provoking story. Transitional space was to appear when she opened up to "as if" and "might be", the first hint of a third dimension and of a possible other place, whether this were to be the past or wishes that were not or could not be acknowledged, above all by herself.

With this opening up she began to take pleasure in playing and it became possible to remember and even recount dreams. But for this to happen, a tolerable relationship needed already to have been created. Three factors therefore converged in the psychodrama configuration: the opportunity that it offered Marie to diffuse her transference because the plurality and diversity of the participants afforded ready-made object splits and made the transference less exciting and less alienating; the constant presence of a third party, which limited the effects of a two-way relationship and served as constant support for the boundaries between self and others; and verification by perception that, despite all her attacks, her objects were not destroyed.

It is interesting to note that psychodrama is not, of course, always a sufficient platform for the task of differentiation, and can also be challenged at any moment. After several months of sessions, Marie seemed to experience all the participants in her psychodrama as a homogeneous whole, working along the same lines and threatening her balance: "You enjoy looking for complicated things that I don't think. You are doing it on purpose to annoy me and make me sick", she would shout at us, sometimes in tears. And this at a point when the very fact of her participation showed that she could not have been completely unaware of the reality of transferential links. It was by accepting transgression of the rule that it should be the patient who proposes and acts a scene that we got through this impasse. In doing this, we accepted that she was taking control of the situation, and we created a new difference by accepting doing everything in her stead. Thus the situation was reversed: like myself in my capacity as play leader, she did not play but watched the others play. Paradoxically, this distancing let her get closer to me, and probably, thanks to that support, to move forward again in primary identification. Any attempt at interpretation would have had the opposite effect. It would have reinforced Marie's feeling that she was being manipulated and that we had control over her internal world. In this type of patient, intolerance of interpretation increases in proportion to the size of their expectations, which reinforces the feeling of loss of boundaries. One is often faced with what J.-B. Pontalis called "incest between psychical apparatuses", which produces in response a strengthening of negativism and a negative therapeutic reaction (Pontalis, 1981).

With Marie, movement in primary identification was helped by assurance that the object would remain external and was neither being destroyed nor confused with an internal object that protected her ego from confusional and persecutory invasion by the object. This external relay brought her internal object under partial control through a process inverse to hallucination, whereby what has been abolished inside reappears outside. Her object's reassuring presence outside gradually allowed her to recognize her internal object and to resume bearable exchanges in play. As is the case in efforts to symbolize, the external object is reassuring because it at once represents the internal object and is sufficiently different from it, even if only on account of its particular perceptual properties. Conversely, as Roussillon (1991) underlined, if "the object" found outside is "too similar to the object represented internally", it is the latter that "is found in danger of being destroyed inside or dragged outside and seduced by the external object".

However, because of the transference and the intensity of the cathexes that it mobilizes, a single external object can prove insufficient and become dangerously confused with the internal object. The presence of several therapists has potential for restarting a preliminary process of differentiation. In psychoanalytic psychodrama, the arrangement of scenes and the constant presence of co-therapists ensure the permanence of a third-party onlooker in self-evidently symmetrical interchanges: the leader watches scenes that are played but holds back from playing, and the co-therapists help, watch, and listen to commentaries that are offered by the leader outside of scenes in his conversations with the patient. "Within Oedipal triangulation this third-party observation performs an essential scopic function in the distinction it forges between the thinking subject and the subject who sees himself thinking: the other person's gaze reflects back the sense of looking at the self and thereby lays foundations for the process of reflection" (Chabert, 1997).

Here we see the effect of re-actualizing primary identifications authorized by a transferential revival of primary homosexuality that has become bearable and non-invasive, thanks to the presence of an external third party.

But, outside of psychodrama, it is important for care settings as a whole to be thought of and used as potential sources of figurative support (which will need decoding) for internal realities that fight shy of representation.

The psychoanalytic model of mental functioning and the psychic apparatus does therefore permit use to be made of external space, and hence of the care setting, with a view to restoring internal psychic space to working order. Its validity can certainly be challenged in so far as, with this approach, the existence of processes that are not manifest is being inferred from information drawn from more explicit situations that I see as having paradigmatic value. However, its validity seems justified by its tendency to get things moving, especially when taking charge of adolescents. I have therefore repeatedly emphasized the importance of the third-party function of this organization of external reality, its role in managing object distance and in balancing narcissism and object relations, as well as its possible function in differentiating and restoring the ego's boundaries and faltering identity. This has led me to advocate bi- and multi-focal therapies as a privileged means of safeguarding psychotherapeutic work with difficult adolescents, by giving concrete expression in external reality to the separation between the setup of external reality represented by the referent and the progressive recognition of an internal reality that takes material shape in the private and protected space of the psychotherapeutic relationship (Jeammet, 1992).

If it preserves its vitality—something that is never fully achieved nor constantly maintained—this tool could be absorbed into psychiatric practice in a range of different ways, and thereby profoundly alter its nature. This would happen because if the demand of classic psychiatry is to work towards isolating target disorders, the distinctive tool of psychoanalysis—while not ignoring the specific consequences of a given disorder—seeks to define it, as Widlöcher (1995) astutely remarked, not in terms of its difference from another disorder but "in terms of its complementarity" and "its function as part of a whole". The whole thus construed is "a type of mental functioning", and what is identified is "an assemblage of operations that organize themselves together". A psychoanalytic outlook allows conduct not to be reduced "to simple sign value", in contrast with the classic psychiatric approach "which does not seek to connect signs with one another" because "it takes them for expressions of an underlying disorder". How can we give full meaning to an adolescent's psychiatric pathology, above all with its implications for his future, without at least trying to connect it with the mental work that is required to cope with the tasks and obligatory need for change that lie ahead of him?

CHAPTER THREE

The influence of psychic trauma on adolescence and its disorders

Dimitris Anastasopoulos

The psychoanalytic and psychiatric literature concerning the creation and development of psychic trauma is extensive and covers a wide range of approaches and interpretations. In this chapter, I deal with the generation of trauma in adolescence, exploring the extent to which this is a period of particular vulnerability to trauma and examining the impact that early or recent psychic traumatization can have on the disturbances that occur during adolescence.

Theoretical review

It is well known that the concept of psychic trauma was originally developed by Sigmund Freud (Freud, 1895d) and involved the attribution of symptoms to the influence of an external event and in particular of the occurrence of sexual seduction of the child. The trauma itself, infantile sexuality, and the libido theory were seen as supplementary and coexisting concepts and also as significant or even decisive factors in the disturbance of the individual and in the degree of his psychic vulnerability (Freud, 1914d). Initially, Freud explained trauma as an imbalance of psychic energy resulting from a rupture, caused by intense excitation, in the protective shield of the ego (Freud, 1920g).

Freud later expanded his theory of trauma, associating it with an experience of the ego as incapable, helpless, and unable to face reality when it has to deal with internal or external stimuli that exert excessive pressure upon it (Freud, 1926d [1925]). Apart from external threats, Freud added losses (of the object or of its love, protection, and care) to the list of traumatogenic factors. The model of trauma thus became more complex, including among the generative factors components of fantasy as well as reality. However, the nucleus of the revival of oedipal fantasies remained unchanged.

Greenacre (1967) saw trauma as an inseparable part of normal development and connected the traumatogenic influence of an event with the individual's developmental stage and with the intensity and quality of the stimulus. She also noted that the development of fixation and, consequently, of vulnerability to the next traumatizing stimulus, or to a repetition of the earlier one, is associated not only with the fantasy or the external event, but also with its confirmation in the form of a traumatizing experience.

Subsequent developmental studies have demonstrated that factors that have a negative impact on psycho-emotional development also tend to increase the vulnerability of the ego to traumatization (Furst, 1986). Constitutional factors, fixations, regression, and the inhibition of ego and superego development have a similar effect. The trauma itself is capable of having a significant influence on the process of affective development.

Edith Jacobson (1959) sees psychic trauma as a narcissistic disorder within the ego involving conflicts between different representations of the self. Her views have been followed by other American analysts, including Bach and Schwartz (1972), who believe that the conflict takes place within the ego between a representation of the self organized around a pathogenic childhood fantasy and a non-traumatic representation of the self.

Krystal (1971), who worked with former detainees in Nazi concentration camps, distinguished between the "near-trauma" and the "catastrophic trauma". In the former, the personality is not overwhelmed, though forms of psychopathology can be triggered. In the latter, the entire personality is flooded and the individual enters a state of overall despair which can lead to permanent psychic damage. Krystal perceives the trauma as a potential or actual state of subjective anguish and disorganization which is connected with some emergency and mobilizes defence mechanisms to deal with the overwhelming feelings flooding the individual. He formed a theory of trauma as a subjective experience determined either by psychic reality or by its unconscious meaning.

Bergmann and Jucovy (1982) drew attention to the significance for the development of psychic trauma of previously existing reality and of the fragility of an immature ego.

Kelman (1946) describes trauma as the individual's unconscious feeling that he has failed to measure up to an idealized self-image. Ulman and Brothers (1988) use a study of cases of rape, war, and incest as the basis for seeing all traumas as narcissistic, acquiring, for the individual, the meaning of the demolition and false reconstruction of archaic narcissistic fantasies. The traumatization thus depends on the degree to which an event attacks the existing archaic narcissistic fantasies, which are central to the organization and maintenance of the self-image.

Blum (1986) argues that the pre-oedipal developmental structure or phase is more vulnerable to traumatization. He distinguishes between acute psychic traumas and states of strain caused by contrary life experiences or damaging developmental factors. Strain involves pathogenic components acting on a chronic basis, distorted modes of development, predisposition, and vulnerability. Blum believes that it is possible for strain to function as a background facilitating the development of acute trauma and that it may also have long-term latent effects. The concept of the cumulative trauma developed by Masud Khan (1974) is close to that of the state of strain.

Sandler (1989) examines the states of strain that each individual inevitably faces during the course of development, and he describes a wide range of factors that contribute to the creation of states of strain or psychic trauma and may ultimately have a decisive impact on psychic evolution.

Psychic trauma: definition and distinctions

Psychic trauma, the traumatic event, the process of traumatization, and the phenomenology of trauma—these are qualities that are often not differentiated with precision, possibly thereby causing confusion (Sandler, Dreher, & Drew, 1991). On the one hand, psychic trauma is an experience with distinctive internal and external features which causes a disturbance in the psychic balance of the psyche, which the self is unable to contain and integrate and to which the self cannot find an organized reply. It is a kind of rupture, a temporary state of disorganization, after which the individual's psychic world is not as it was before. Psychological balance and functionality can be restored, but the trauma is now—as an entity—part of the overall internal structure of the subject. On the other hand, the words "traumatic" or "traumatogenic" can be used to describe an event, an experience, or an internal or external stimulus that, by acting acutely, cumulatively, or chronically, can assume the dimensions of a trauma as it is experienced by the individual. Sudden severe losses, massive disasters, and extreme or prolonged conditions of psychic pressure can function traumatically for most people. On the individual level, there is an almost infinite variety of potentially traumatic events.

The quantity, duration, and quality of the external stimulus/event are among the factors that can affect traumatization, and a role is also played by the stability of the individual's psychic structure, the stage of emotional development, the completion of maturation, the integrity of internal objects, and the resolution of internal conflicts. When the environment is supportive, it seems to contribute to the avoidance of traumatization.

However, we should distinguish such potentially traumatizing stimuli from those that are "objectively" traumatogenic, in the sense that they would cause psychic trauma in the majority of those who experienced them, such as extreme instances of massively destructive intrusions into the human psyche. On the other hand, the degree to which a permanently traumatic area is created depends on the subject's internal psychic condition, as does the subject's ability to recover from the trauma.

Since, therefore, the traumatogenic event has to be internalized (i.e. to be linked with internal fantasies, images, objects, and representations, or even with conflict-vulnerable parts of the psyche or with traumatogenic experiences or psychic traumas of the past), it can be hypothesized that each psychic trauma refers to a revival of early experiences and traumas. The question thus arises of whether there can be such things as "new" traumas after early childhood.

However, to state that each new experience is linked with earlier experiences and triggers affects and associations is certainly not to eradicate the significance and uniqueness of the experience or to overlook the importance of the numerous internal and external factors that effect the final form of the experience. This enables us to talk of traumas that occur in early childhood and also of traumas that take place in present time—despite the fact that both kinds of trauma are related to the individual background, early experiences, and personal history of each subject.

In order for a psychic trauma to occur, it seems necessary that (a) the subject is in a particular relationship with the external or internal object, and (b) that the environment is perceived as hostile or incapacitating. The consequences are (a) a rupture in the individual's psychological protective shield, (b) massive regression and confusion as to the distinction between reality and fantasy, and (c) a feeling in the individual of being unprotected against the emergence of archaic anxieties and, in particular, of annihilation anxiety.

Adolescence is a developmental stage that the emergence and re-working of early experiences, in conjunction with an unstable identity and self-image, make vulnerable to the development of traumas capable of leading to emotional disorders. It follows that the contribution made by traumatogenic situations to the development of psychopathology in adolescence may be the result either of early psychic traumas or of more recent ones. In this chapter, my focus is on the latter instance, which usually attracts less attention, and I attempt to demonstrate its connection with developmental phases and with the disorders of adolescence.

The vulnerability of adolescents to psychic trauma

To begin with, adolescence itself is usually seen as a stage of

1. intensification in the sexual and aggressive instincts;
2. regression to earlier stages in psycho-emotional development;
3. the revival of unresolved conflicts;
4. intensification of narcissism and fantasies of omnipotence;
5. fluidity in the sense of the boundaries of the self and of the body-image;
6. the search for an identity;
7. mourning for the loss of the childhood self and for dependence on the parental objects.

It is not hard to remember how frequently adolescents can be "hurt" by affective situations, which assume huge proportions within them against the background of emotional uncertainty and narcissism. We also know that they frequently display identity disorders, confusion, impulsive behaviour, and acting out caused by an inability to work through intense emotions; the concept of time may expand or contract subjectively for them, and intense psychosomatic phenomena often appear. Perhaps it is no coincidence that all these features are also components of post-traumatic stress disorder (PTSD).

In PTSD, we distinguish two broad categories of trauma:

I. The trauma that is the result of a single, sudden blow.

II. The trauma that is the outcome of prolonged or repeated exposure to the traumatizing event.

The characteristics of the second category are a dulling of the affects, rage, and unrelenting sadness. Children and adolescents with traumas of the first category have clear memories of the event, perceptual disorders, and a tendency constantly to explore why and how the event occurred. Guilt manifests itself in both cases. There are cases in which a psychic trauma may begin as a Type I event and continue with the addition of a Type II trauma, such as a sudden loss of the parents (Terr, 1991).

The symptoms and phenomena observed in such cases have been described by many authors and are summarized by Terr (1983, 1985, 1987) as follows:

1. cognitive–perceptual difficulties, initially resulting in hallucinations, delusions, misperceptions, and memory disorders, which can last for years;
2. collapse of the developmental achievements already made, focusing on a removal of autonomy and of the feeling that the child is able to affect his own life (the phenomena here are a reduction of the time perspective, unconscious efforts towards "reparation", a sense of foreknowledge of the future, and a guilty feeling of responsibility);
3. repetition compulsion, with repetition of the traumatic event (in play or nightmares), repetition through acting out, and re-enactments.

Although differences in level of development, sociocultural background, family psychopathology, pre-existent psychic vulnerabilities, and relations with the community have a long-term effect on the severity of PTSD and on the qualities in which the trauma finds expression, there is a striking similarity to the features and symptoms displayed by children and adolescents (Terr, 1985). Furthermore, the traumas of childhood and adolescence—unlike those of adulthood—are never forgotten, perhaps because they were incorporated into the psychic structure during development.

Is adolescence itself, one wonders, a potentially traumatic experience? If we accept the view that the trauma, as an event in psychic life, may even have the effect of fostering maturation, then it is possible to see adolescence *per se* as a traumatic experience. However, the answer depends on the broader or narrower theoretical definition one selects (Cooper, 1986), but it does seem that adolescence can be a developmental phase in which the individual is vulnerable to psychic traumas.

In adolescence, many of the psychic processes are "open-ended" in the sense that they are being redefined, reorganized, and re-examined. Among examples of this situation are the adolescent's uncertainty and quest for identity and purpose. The emergence of internal conflicts and drives seeking integration into a new framework for interaction and the relationship with internal and external objects leaves the adolescent in a vulnerable position. The renegotiation of the relationship with the parental objects on which the adolescent is dependent and the gradual establishment of substantive relationships with external (non-narcissistic) objects combine to form what is in essence a process of inside/outside internalization and introjective identification/externalization, and projective identification. The rapid changes that come about in the appearance and functions of the body with the onset of puberty fragment the body image, which has to be reconstructed and internalized as part of the self-image for a sense of control over what is happening inside and outside the adolescent's body to be established.

The weakening of ego functions, reduced toleration of frustrations, and restriction of the breadth and flexibility of defences caused by regression, the often inadequate reality testing (under the influence of intense fantasies and daydreams and of a sense of being unable to cope without the relationship of dependency on the parental figures), and the inability to withstand the pressure from the superego combine to create a background of lowered resistance to traumatic states (Furst, 1986).

The occurrence of an extreme event does not in itself constitute a psychic trauma, in the sense that it does not produce pathogenic effects until its memory is linked, in the psyche, with the appropriate representations. An instance of infant abuse, for instance, will become traumatic when it becomes possible to use it developmentally (Baranger, Baranger, & Mom, 1988)—in other words, when it undergoes retroactive causation of the past to the present. If the trauma takes place on two different time levels (on an external/perceptual level and on an internal/fantasy level), then both the event and the regression necessary for its traumatic dimension are required, resulting in regression of the ego to previous stages. Seen in this light, an event can easily take on traumatogenic proportions if there has already been a traumatizing stimulus, large or small. Furthermore, seen from the angle of the "second chance" of adolescence (Blos, 1967), it is easier during adolescence to reconstruct an earlier trauma if the environment is suitable or if therapeutic help is available.

Khan (1974) developed the concept of the cumulative trauma caused by the mother's failure to function as a protective shield for the child. He argues that the bond that develops between them is based on a projective and incorporative identification that interpolates itself into each assimilation and introjection of new object representations and functions as a psychic organizing factor. The breaches in the care-taking role come to the surface in dramatic form during adolescence, when the mother is rejected and the process of psychic integration may seem impossible to the adolescent.

The intensity of the adolescent's sexual (incestuous) and destructive fantasies predisposes him to receive an externally destructive event or a sexual violation as a trauma. This is particularly true if the event is capable of gratifying an inner fantasy and causing it to "come true" (de Saussure, 1982). The sense of defencelessness and helplessness may function in connection with latent destructive anxieties to make the traumatic experience a permanent source of regression and inhibition of development for the adolescent.

Sexual abuse against a background of incestuous and bisexual fantasies (and, on a deeper level, of pre-genital fantasies of merging and fusion with the object) may function traumatically, often leading to permanent sexual incapacity or deviation (Krell & Okin, 1984; Marvasti, 1986).

Susceptibility to psychic trauma during adolescence

The individual's degree of vulnerability to the trauma and its consequences will depend largely on the period of life and development during which the event occurs (Neubauer, 1980). Most authors agree that an external event or series of events has to be linked with inner processes and with the quality of the subject's object-cathected relations before it can constitute a trauma (Sandler et al., 1991). I think that we can distinguish two categories of trauma which may occur in adolescence. The first is particularly applicable to adolescence, and consists of (a) cumulative trauma, (b) traumatic sequences of events happening in the present, (c) associative trauma (in the sense of the associative connection of current events with events in the past which did not by themselves have a traumatic effect), and (d) acute exogenous trauma (in the sense of the experiencing of conditions so extreme that they would cause psychic trauma in the vast majority of adolescents, such as states of massive disaster and loss or a prolonged life-threat which cannot be avoided or reacted against). The second category, which may also occur in adolescence, consists of (a) revival of childhood trauma, (b) re-enacted trauma from an earlier period of life, (c) trauma superimposed upon a favourable background (in the sense of isolated events that ultimately have a traumatic outcome because of the particular developmental state reached by the individual or of the individual's relations with his internal objects), and (d) the "pure" trauma (the existence of which is questionable).

Muses (1978) identifies two factors that may provide protection against potentially traumatic experiences: satisfactory or high self-esteem, and the sense of belonging to a group in which the individual feels good. When talking about adolescence, we should bear in mind the extent to which the self-image—and, consequently, self-esteem—is tested when those conditions are absent. The sense of containment that the adolescent seeks in the peer group may provide protection, but it also exposes the adolescent to disillusionment when it becomes apparent that his peers are more fragile than the parental figures. Bessel and Van der Kolk (1985) studied the syndrome of psychic trauma subsequent to the death of a fellow-soldier in the Vietnam War, noting the disorganization and rage caused in the adolescent soldier by the loss of his narcissistic twin, together with a desire for revenge and indifference to danger. A resort to fantasies of omnipotence is one defence against the extreme psychic pain of the trauma. Psychically traumatized individuals experience themselves as having had their internal objects destroyed (Tracey, 1991). In adolescence, the developmentally appropriate regressive swings can combine with a potentially traumatic event to create permanent regression and a trauma by overcoming the psychic defences (Furst, 1986). Adolescents are particularly vulnerable to states such as object loss, passive dependency, loss of control, and reduced self-esteem (Blos, 1962). These events can be seen either as fertile ground for the creation of a trauma or as superimposing themselves on earlier traumas. The formation of a stable personality in late adolescence can be achieved when residual traumas (Blos, 1968) are incorporated into the structure of the individual's character (Furst, 1986).

McDougall (1986) writes that the meaning of an event determines its traumatic nature. As a result, the meaning that adolescents attach to the way in which others perceive them—in general, or in connection with the question of sexuality—is a constant source of potentially traumatic experiences. Traumatized adolescents become involved in acting out the conflict rather than storing it in the memory and gradually working it psychically, which might permit the trauma to be overcome. Acting out often remains as a permanent characteristic incorporated into the adolescent's personality.

Adolescence resembles a series of consecutive psychic ruptures and disorganizations which can be balanced. It could also be described as a series of traumas that have been reconstructed and, under normal conditions, do not accumulate. In other words, when the internal objects are more or less intact and the ego relatively mature, the individual's own psyche undertakes the task of reconstruction and, consequently, the process of emerging from and developing beyond the fragility and confusion of adolescence. It seems to be the case that the reconstructions, not the traumas, normally accumulate into a whole during adolescence.

Casement (1987) uses the theory of Matte Blanco (1975) in order to argue that traumatic experiences associate with one another as unconscious sets, which, despite the fact that they were not experienced simultaneously, can be linked regardless of quality and time, thus reinforcing the trauma and bringing it to the surface. These unconscious sets of experiences, mobilized by similar experiences in the present, can create a delusion of simulation between past and present. This may be a further argument in favour of the view that adolescence is a sequence of traumas and reconstructions.

In the psychically traumatized individual, distinctions between objects, places, and times are lost, while the ego undergoes massive regression and the id is incapable of distinguishing qualities and objects. The emotional experience cannot be experienced, worked through, or psychically integrated. It functions destructively, wrecking psychic adjustments and resistances and creating a chaotic sense of inability and absence of support from internal and external objects, resulting in a massive regression. The barriers between reality and fantasy collapse. The psychically traumatized individual experiences pain, but not what he is suffering; he is flooded by the pain and *within it*, rather that it being *within him* (Bion, 1977). If we accept the view of "silent" pre-traumatic time or of the unassimilated "absolute" trauma of infancy, which is experienced and perceived as a trauma during the historical development of the individual (Baranger et al., 1988), then perhaps the sequence of traumas and their activation may occur more frequently in adolescence. The condensation of time and the quest for cause and purpose which are characteristic of adolescence, may, in conjunction with regression, constitute the appropriate conditions for the development of an active trauma.

The personal history of each individual may contain potentially traumatic events that function as landmarks in development and are the result of frustrations in object relationships (Le Guen, 1982). As a stage involving the renegotiation and reconstruction of the individual's history, adolescence marks and activates events, dramatizing experiences under the influence of the regression and superegotic attitudes of adolescents (Glick & Meyers, 1988).

Adolescence manifests itself in a sharply psychosocial manner, in which the central position is occupied by the search for answers in connection with the individual's object relationships. Perhaps the strong sense of shame observed during this period is its most characteristic feature. By definition, trauma involves the existence of an object—internal or external—and it is often triggered by social factors. This leads to thoughts about the extent to which the trauma of the parents or other close relatives may "infect" the adolescent; about how far the cultural and social environment (living conditions, oppression, acceptance, support network, etc: Blum, 1986, p. 27) is capable of traumatizing across a wide spectrum, from indirect or direct humiliation and assaults on the adolescent's self-esteem to severe and massive losses; about how far the history of the people to which the adolescent belongs may function as a medium for the revival or perpetuation of "national traumas", which become interwoven with the individual's personal history; and, ultimately, about the degree to which, in different cultural settings, there may be significant differences in the events that can be traumatogenic.

The influence of psychic trauma on adolescent disorders

I think that we can distinguish three categories in the significance and impact of psychic trauma in adolescents:

1. *Recent psychic traumas,* which have occurred during the course of adolescence and are associated mainly with the particular features of this phase of development and its primary objectives. Such traumas may, for example, be connected with a physical defect or difference, a sudden and important loss, rejection by the peer group or failure to bond with it, social exclusion (emigration, racism, classification as a scapegoat), abandonment, shame as a result of disillusionment, or insults to their sexuality (seduction, rape, incest). The degree to which these events will function traumatically is certainly connected with the stability of the individual's psychic structure and his previous experiences. However, they seem to result in disorders that are mainly characteristic of this specific developmental phase and tend to be relatively easier to reverse (e.g. acting out, delinquent acts, identity disorders, hypochondriac and psychosomatic symptoms, depressive impulses).

Example I

Laura was referred to me by another psychiatrist when she was 17 years old, for an identity disorder with signs of depersonalization, intense and disorganizing anxiety, and a question as to the onset of a psychotic syndrome.

Laura was born in Lebanon to an Italian father and a Christian Lebanese mother. She was sent to a French school, as was customary for the children of prosperous families. When the civil war broke out, the family moved to Greece and Laura registered at an American college. As a result, Laura spoke Italian in the family, Arabic when talking to her mother, and English at college. By not speaking Greek, she felt excluded from making friends.

In our sessions, it soon became apparent that Laura's ego structure was relatively solid. Her relationship with her mother was intensely ambivalent. The picture she conveyed of her family was of a pluralistic set of heterogeneous components: her comparatively good relations with her parents, the presence of friends in the peer group, and a cosmopolitan environment that accepted such situations seem to have had a containing effect.

When the family moved to Greece, the multiracial, polyglot elements emerged strongly on the surface. The support of the peer group to which Laura felt she belonged was suddenly removed, and conflicts developed in the parental relationship. It was as if the environment was no longer able to contain events, and cracks had appeared in the defensive shield. Laura felt strange and alien towards everything. In her anxiety to hold on to something, she developed a relationship with a Palestinian, a move that was greeted with rage from her father over this affair with a potential "terrorist" and with contempt from her mother towards a man who may have been an Arab but was also a Muslim.

Laura had an intense need for containment to enable her to reassemble the parts of herself that she felt to have been shattered "as if there had suddenly been an explosion". In the process of psychotherapy, the traumatic "rift" of the move to Greece, which had been perceived as the uprooting and fracturing of the personality, was healed. Laura passed her college examinations, stabilized her relations with a circle of friends, and successfully claimed her independence from her parents.

A year after the end of therapy, Laura came to my office to express her gratitude for the help she had received. Everything appeared to be normal.

Example II

Michael was referred for psychoanalytic psychotherapy when he was 16 years old. Since the age of 13, he had been withdrawn from his peer group and had avoided engaging in social contact of any kind. His performance at school was growing constantly worse, and he had outbursts of rage directed mainly to his mother. In the very first session, he disclosed that he had considered suicide, and that one night the previous month he had spent half an hour on a second-floor windowsill, ambivalent as to whether he was going to jump or not.

Michael had grown up in a prosperous environment. His father, a university graduate, had an immature, narcissistic personality with masochistic elements, and in the past he had taken antidepressant medication for a short time. The mother, also a graduate, was attractive, dynamic at work, and insecure in her personal relationships. The relationship between the parental couple was always ambivalent, with intense conflicts and mutual rejection.

Michael's father had projected strongly into him an ego ideal with high expectations, while at the same time passing up no opportunity of competing with his son and humiliating him in order to boost his own low self-esteem. The mother was indecisive and discontented with life and her relationship, relying indirectly on Michael to supplement her emotional deprivation. Michael remembered with pain scenes in which he had been humiliated by his father or in which the parents had rowed—scenes that usually ended with the parents deciding to stay together "for the boy's sake". He also recalled the paralysing anxiety he felt each time he had to confront their expectations of him. Nonetheless, he grew up normally, performing well in sports and in the classroom and integrating smoothly into the peer group.

When he was 13, he listened in on the telephone extension and was terribly shocked to hear his mother flirting with a young man who was among the close family friends. The emotions that surged up in him were associated with incestuous fantasies and anxiety about his mother, mixed with revulsion and rage. He also felt rage and disgust towards the humble, dependent attitude adopted by his father, who Michael felt was incapable of intervening. This had the effect of disorganizing his defences. His predominant feeling was one of unbearable shame, which took the form of anxiety that other people might see and understand the dirty, worthless things he concealed within himself.

Michael found it very difficult to trust the psychotherapeutic process and to "expose" himself. The role played by the repeated humiliations, frustrations, projective identifications, and ambivalent relationships with his parents was revealed little by little. The incident with the overheard telephone conversation, to which more evidence of the mother's extramarital activities was later added, functioned as a catalytic trauma in Michael's psyche, activating all the traumatogenic experiences of the past. Before long, he reached balance in therapy, dealt satisfactorily with his parents' divorce, and went to university in another part of the country, where he is now a successful student.

2. *Earlier "silent" traumas* or latent traumatic areas in the psyche, which become connected by association with recent experiences that by themselves would not be traumatizing. Traumas of this kind seem to lead to disturbances that are more severe (e.g. anorexia, bulimia) and which, while they may be specific to adolescence or not, nonetheless have a high incidence in adolescence (e.g. depression, suicide attempts, substance abuse).

Example III

Anna was referred at the age of 15 years (by a teacher from her school) for anorexia nervosa. Her parents had separated when she was 8, and she lived with her mother. Her father was a prosperous businessman, with a mild personality and complicated relations with women. Her mother was a housewife (occasionally underemployed), with an immature, narcissistic personality and elements of depression.

From an early point in Anna's life, situations and events had accumulated without assuming the character of a psychic trauma. She grew up in an atmosphere of constant conflict and of insults and frustrations in her relationship with her mother, which became worse after the parents divorced. She had also witnessed scenes of violence between the parents.

The mother's subsequent boyfriend attempted to seduce Anna; when she complained to her mother, the latter blamed her—as she (the mother) did whenever anything went wrong in her life. Anna also experienced neglect of her health by her mother, who behaved negatively and insultingly towards her when the girl entered puberty, and the father's inability to intervene.

Anna thus became a closed and excessively sensitive adolescent. At 14, she manifested the first signs of anorexia nervosa, which the parents handled with prejudice and clumsiness. When she came to me, she had lost 30 per cent of her body weight, was silent, had no friends and was interested only in the theatre. After many fluctuations, we succeeded in establishing a therapeutic relationship. Anna was able to overcome her anorexia, and she developed an admirable degree of insight. Little by little, we managed to work on the accumulated and potentially traumatogenic experiences that in adolescence had crystallized into a specific pathology. "Whenever I received a blow of that kind, I put up with the frustration and the anger—as if I had something to hope for, as if I had no choice anyway. When I went into junior high school, I was in despair at the prospect of always feeling like that and of my relationship with my mother continuing unchanged. Although I didn't realize it at the time, my refusal of food was a way of controlling what I felt inside myself." The atmosphere of regression, intensification of instinctive drives, and sharp emergence of earlier conflicts overcame Anna's ability to contain the traumatogenic experiences she had undergone up to that time. Her hatred for, and competition with, her mother found an outlet in the anorexia nervosa.

3. *Early active traumas,* which have already formulated or left their mark on components of the individual's personality or psychopathology and which, during adolescence, are expressed fully or take their final form (e.g. personality disorders, narcissistic and borderline disorders).

EXAMPLE IV

George, aged 14 years, was referred to me for aggressive behaviour with violent and destructive phenomena, poor performance at school, lack of relationships with his peer group, and occasional thefts of small sums of money from his mother.

The parents had married when the mother became pregnant, although she did not feel ready for such a step. The mother was American; she manifested depression four months after George's birth, and when he was 6 years old she was hospitalized for severe depression.

The father was Greek, a university graduate of a brilliant academic background and career, whose excessive professional commitments meant that, in practice, he was absent. He failed to set limits, and he avoided seeing anything unpleasant.

As an infant, George was hyperactive, whining, and constantly demanding to be picked up. He usually slept in the same bed as his mother, so that his hard-working father could get a good night's sleep. George reacted to the birth of his brother, two years later, by "running away" (he was found two kilometres from the house) and by behaving in an actively hostile manner towards the baby. Nocturnal enuresis continued until the age of 7 years. At the age of 9, he had 20 sessions with a child psychiatrist on his difficulty in developing relations with his peer group. After that time, he had appeared to be adjusting to the environment.

During the assessment sessions, George was taciturn, provocative, aggressive, rejecting, and insecure, frequently resorting to fantasies of omnipotence. At school, the teachers found him difficult to tolerate, and his only relationship with his fellow pupils was on the basketball court. He often destroyed things, and his behaviour towards his brother was frequently violent. The picture was of a behaviour disorder with psychopathic elements against the background of a borderline personality.

George himself identified the family's move from the United States to Greece as the central traumatogenic event in his life; he spoke little Greek, lost the few friends he had made with such difficulty, and felt that he belonged nowhere, that he was not appreciated, and that the promise he had been given—that his father would have more time for him when they moved to Greece—had been broken. During the course of psychotherapeutic work (which required short-term hospitalization in a psychiatric unit on a number of occasions), it was possible to bring to the surface the successive traumatic experiences that had accumulated since early childhood: scenes of psychological violence and rejection between the parents, a suicide attempt on the part of the mother, a period in which George himself had felt that the other people around him in the home were lifeless objects, and the parents' emotional unavailability. It became clear that George had had difficulty in coping with the repeated deprivations and frustrations, and that by the end of latency he had achieved some degree of personality integration. The loss of an environment in which he himself had fought to develop supports, coinciding with his entry into adolescence, assumed the dimensions of an uncounterbalanced trauma.

In these categories, we can see that the severity of the influence of the adolescent trauma can range from minor disturbances connected with recent traumatic events to more severe disorders connected with early traumas. While it seems to be a period of greater vulnerability to psychic trauma, adolescence also possesses greater reserves of the ability to reconstruct and compensate.

Therapy

Tonnesman (1980) advances the view that re-enactment in adolescence is associated with regressive ego states, while acting out involves regressive defences directed towards the instincts. The traumas of childhood, even including those of non-verbal, physically expressed infancy (McDougall, 1986), can be re-enacted in adolescence. The dissociative experiences of infancy led to discontinuity in development and are often re-enacted in adolescence in a state of psychic dissociation. In such situations, the therapist has to function as a supplementary ego to the adolescent rather than interpreting these phenomena as resistance to transference; in the latter case, the therapeutic relationship may function as a repetition of the traumatic experience—that is, of the failure of the adolescent's environment to contain his anxiety and respond to his needs.

Casement (1987) argues that the analytic procedure may prove to be traumatic if the analyst is unable to negotiate elements connected with possible shortcomings in the therapy, or refuses to allow this to take place. Tracey (1991) points out that if the therapist completely ignores the significance of the traumatic event that may have had a traumatic effect, the patient will experience guilt and be unable to contain, emotionally, what he is feeling.

The defence mechanisms mobilized during traumatic states range from the most "primitive" mechanisms (denial, separation, psychosomatic symptoms, avoidance) to others that are relatively "advanced" (suppression, identification, reaction formation, isolation, displacement). Projection does not seem to be used, perhaps because the subject's object relationship is interrupted or damaged because of the trauma and thus its development cannot be conceived.

My own experience indicates that failure to recognize the reality of the traumatic event makes psychotherapeutic psychotherapy of adolescents impossible since (a) it prevents the development of the transference which is necessary for the therapeutic process to advance, and (b) it once more dissociates the traumatic event (object) from the subject. By contrast, an attitude of emotional containment, with acceptance of the patient's own pace where references to the trauma are concerned, facilitation of extensive discussion of the events, and discreet interventions during the first stages in the approach to the subject, can be helpful. Psychotherapy is equally impossible when it deals excessively with the dramatic nature of the external event, reinforcing the defences around the patient's fantasies and in some cases even becoming perversive, in the form of persistent inquiries for details in cases of abuse. I believe that both extremes are a defensive resort by the therapist who splits the inside from the outside when, for reasons of countertransference, he is unable to tolerate an approach to the overall picture. Difficulties in countertransference have, in fact, been reported in the therapy both of Holocaust victims (De Wind, 1984) and of sexually abused children and adolescents (Krell & Okin, 1984; Marvasti, 1986). Such a therapeutic attitude does not allow integration to occur and consequently narrows the scope for the revival and reconstruction of the trauma.

We are familiar with the intensity of the countertransference feelings that are mobilized in psychotherapists working with adolescents (Anastasopoulos & Tsiantis, 1996; Brandell, 1992). When there is also a psychic trauma mobilized by an obvious external cause (disaster, abuse, abandonment, severe loss, etc.), countertransference is sometimes difficult to control and the therapist feels flooded by the intensity of external reality, leaving him little room to recognize and promote the working-through of fantasies associated with the traumatic event. The tendency towards acting out manifested by adolescents is capable of confusing the overall picture by presenting numerous situations as tragic, deadlocked, and thus traumatizing.

The angle from which the psychotherapist views the psychic trauma and his theoretical position will affect the mode of his approach. The hermeneutic definition of the trauma emphasizes the interpretation of the event given by the subject. The therapist is seen as facilitating integration by means of interpretative work, and the significance is attached to the precision and specificity of the interpretation. The developmental definition of trauma stresses the absence, or defectiveness, of the maternal protective shield around the child. Therapists who approach trauma from this angle—or in adaptational terms—underline the significance of the therapist's ability to tolerate the painful emotions and function as a new and caring object in the present (Rothstein, 1986).

Approaches that place most emphasis on the external event itself lie outside the framework of psychoanalytic theories and therapy.

Trauma therapy, regardless of the therapeutic approach, is directed towards reconstruction of the trauma and its psychic integration. This is possible only by means of the revival, in the therapeutic relationship, of the traumatic events or situations. Just as both memory and an object are required for the trauma, so they are needed for the attempt to reconstruct it.

Reconstruction of the trauma involves the recollection and revival of it in a framework that will prevent re-traumatization while promoting the secondary process and integration. This task is usually assigned to therapy, where the precedents are known and can be studied. However, appropriate psychic holding can also be found in the environment outside the psychotherapeutic setting (with, for example, a stable heterosexual relationship, achievements that foster maturation, the peer group, restoration of functional relationships with the parents). Associative emergence of the memory and a desire to answer questions may also take the place of the desire for reparation.

As a result, the entire procedure bears resemblances to the process of mourning: revival of the loss in a therapeutic or favourable/supportive setting; recognition of acceptance of the event as irreversible, and liberation of the ability to invest emotionally in objects; and reparation. Losses that are not mourned can result in trauma or can create a vulnerable area in which the traumatogenic event is temporarily balanced. The mourning of the loss permits the reconstruction of the trauma, minimizing its psychologically toxic effect and leaving room for the mobilization of psychic forces for reparation.

The last word has certainly not been said about psychic trauma—or about adolescence and its disturbances. My intention in this chapter has been to cast a little light on the processes of adolescence in connection with traumatic experiences. It might be useful to continue with an exploration of the mechanisms that have a protective effect on the psychic equilibrium of adolescents in traumatogenic situations and of the impact made by the personality and theoretical position of the therapist on the process of reconstructing the psychic trauma. However, I believe that acknowledgement and understanding of the traumatic area and experience increases our prognostic skills and the effectiveness of our psychotherapeutic approach.

CHAPTER FOUR

Containment and the body of the analyst: on psychotic transference in adolescence. A case of dysmorphophobia

Julia Pestalozzi

In this chapter, I would like to share my thoughts on psychotic transference, which—as I have learned over the years while losing a bit of my fear of it—is, to my mind, the chance *par excellence* in the therapeutic encounter with the psychotic patient.

I should like to show that florid psychotic phases (with or without delusional transference) within an otherwise bland, quiet pathology can be viewed as a therapeutically prepared and even sometimes wished-for chance for structural rearrangement—on condition, of course, that it is professionally contained and answered and "dualized", as Gaetano Benedetti would put it. It is regrettable that so often in psychiatry a defence is set up against the joint psychotic experience. Freud's dictum about the symptom that disappears in the melting-pot of transference also applies to delusional transference. Herbert Rosenfeld draws a similar conclusion, as does Benedetti, to whom I am greatly indebted for

---

A theoretically extended and partly different version of this chapter was published in *Kinderanalyse, 1996, 4* (1), under the title "Psychotische Übertragung als Chance".

shaping my thinking and who taught me to find meaning in the apparently meaningless.

I try to demonstrate these ideas here with a purely clinical vignette of a case of dysmorphophobia, a condition that has a certain aura through the Wolf Man (Freud, 1918b [1914]) but is otherwise rare and peculiar, with an extremely bad prognosis, and on the whole is considered intractable (Pestalozzi, 1988, 1996). A short review of the psychopathology of dysmorphophobia is given at the end of this chapter.

Since dysmorphophobia is clinically a delusion about the deformation of one part of the body (usually the nose, chin, ears, sometimes breast or penis), it highlights how mental representations of our bodies can represent a distorted perception of a fragmented self.

However, I assume that all of us—not only the overtly psychotic—are unconsciously, or partly consciously, imbued with infantile, fantastic images of the insides and outsides of our bodies. These unconscious images of our bodies suffuse not only what is obvious—our sexual and other relations—but also our more abstract ideas, particularly regarding human relations (e.g. our theory on *containing*: the way we cathect this ideal). This assumption is not meant to invalidate our theoretical framework. On the contrary, it gives our theory flesh and blood, allows it to be cathected, to be reflected on, and thus we are able work with it. The case study and the therapy presented here should serve to exemplify these ideas.

* * *

Before discussing the case, I would like to identify the theoretical sources that have influenced my technique for treating psychotic, particularly schizophrenic, patients. I have to admit to a certain "multilingualism" in my approach.

It is not possible in this chapter to summarize Benedetti's great oeuvre. In his view, a central motif of the schizophrenic patient is ego-loss, along with a (often also explicit) death experience; there is also the patient's lack of ability to position himself between the extremes of object-hunger and object-fear. Benedetti, who is clearly not a representative of pure "ego-psychology", takes as his starting point Federn's (1952) classic concept of psychosis as a loss of ego boundaries. Benedetti rejects conflict theory for schizophrenics, referring to the experience that psychotic patients can seldom integrate interpretations in the usual psychoanalytic sense. The key words in his technique are (a) the intense identification with the existential distress of the patient in his "death landscape", and (b) the therapeutic fantasy that first enables the therapist "to communicate with the patient within the symptom . . . i.e. within the limits of the security the symptom demands. . . . [Often there are] no conflict knots to untie, rather it is more important to fill up the existential emptiness" (Benedetti, 1983, p. 73 [all quotations from Benedetti translated for this edition]). To do this, the therapist must deeply and actively identify with the generally unimaginable distress of the patient and must also allow her therapeutic fantasy to operate in order to give the patient's symptoms—whose language the therapist learns to understand—a kind of "rotation". This is what Benedetti's concept of *positivization* refers to:

> A kind of "rotation" of the symptom within the interpersonal relationship takes place and through the therapist's comments it becomes a second sight. . . . Such a change in quality makes it possible for the patient to get in touch with his symptom so that he can work through it. . . .
>
> The patient, for example, feels "influenced" by a human being. The therapist replies that this experience of being influenced is a sign of his special "sensitivity". The transference of the word sensitivity in the pathological sense into the word meaning general human sensitivity does not take place in playing with the word which has two so painfully different experiences at its heart, but in the fact that the therapist believes in the patient's sensitivity, on an opening up of the unconscious which is often so typical for schizophrenic patients and represents the "creative" aspect of the illness. [Benedetti, 1983, pp. 73–74]

Although, along with a phenomenological point of view and much inspired by the *"réalisation symbolique"* of Sechehaye (1951), Benedetti's theory is supported by a broadly based psychoanalytic theory, his technique rests on trying to fill up the existential emptiness that the *a priori* assumed ego-loss has caused. The components of this courageous technique include immersion in the patient's symbol language, "positivization" of his images by their metamorphosis in the therapeutic fantasy, the therapist's explicit offer to "want to accompany his/her patient in the death landscape", and the therapist's just wanting to be with the patient.

Turning now to the Kleinian and post-Kleinian view (Rosenfeld, Bion, Segal, Meltzer, etc.), this contrasts profoundly with the idea of an *a priori* psychological deficit of the ego. Rather, the ego-disturbance is considered more as the

> expression of powerful defence activities ... springing from a deep-seated dread of destructiveness ... (death instinct) ... the potential schizophrenic ... makes excessive use of primitive defence mechanisms in order to protect ... his primary object, the nurturing mother. ... Excessive use of projective identification distorts perception, leads to confusion between self and object, internal and external reality, predisposes to concrete thinking. [Jackson, 1992, pp. 39–40]

This leads to a disruption in symbolization and, in fact, weakens the ego. Segal's and Bion's revolutionary work demonstrates how the so-called psychotic part of the personality deforms the thinking process: driven by envy and the desire to be able to avoid the pain that the separateness of the object produces, the psychotic self attacks any thinking that points to human need or to healthy dependence. Kleinian and post-Kleinian technique is based on the existence of the left-overs of the "non-psychotic part of the self" and its wish to be understood (epistemophily, "K" function). Interpretation (although, in modern technique, a "not-too-early" interpretation) is the key. "Holding" and "containing" exist here in the form of comprehending and making comprehensible.

The case study discussed in this chapter demonstrates how these concepts shaped my thinking about my patient and how I made use of this technique.

H. F. Searles, one of the great authors on schizophrenic therapy, with immense clinical experience, has done much work with Kleinian epistemology, but his therapeutic ideal is different—in fact, it is similar to Benedetti's in many respects. Searles' way of thinking and working provided me with fundamental and guiding principles:

> Transference as we see it in the neurotic patient implies three whole persons—the patient, the therapist, and the person who

> figured in the person's early life. The schizophrenic patient has never solidly achieved a level of ego-differentiation and ego-integration which will allow him to experience three whole persons, or even two whole persons, or, as yet, one whole person. The question of whether he will ever achieve such a level of ego-maturation will depend, more than anything else—in so far as the therapist's contribution is concerned—upon the latter's capacity to perform three tasks. First, the therapist must become able to function as a part of the patient and to permit the patient to be genuinely, at a deep level of psychological functioning, a part of himself. Secondly, he must be able to foster the patient's individuation (and, to a not insignificant degree his own re-individuation) out of this level of relatedness, a level which is conceptualised. . . as being a phase of symbiotic relatedness between patient and doctor. The therapist's third task is to discern and make interpretations concerning the patient's now differentiated and now integrated whole object, that is to say neurotic, kind of transference manifestations. . . . What was formerly in him a transference psychosis is now a transference neurosis. [Searles, 1965, pp. 661–662]

Intensive psychotherapy with psychotics poses a very personal challenge to analysts, and we would do well to use a theory and a technique that closely corresponds to our own structure, our own residual neurosis, perhaps even our "psychotic core". I think, if we are to be serious, that this is not only legitimate but also reasonable. Searles and Rosenfeld taught us how much and how unavoidably the psychotherapy of psychotics stimulates fantasies of omnipotence and helplessness (Rosenfeld, 1987, p. 8). If we do not try to come close to our own "psychotic core" during and after personal analysis, I think such work would, to my mind, be "wild" and hardly answerable.

Case history

About twelve years ago, "Florian", a handsome, utterly despairing, morose, and trapped 16-year-old boy, was brought to me by his parents. When we were alone, he told me that his life, his future, were ruined because of his horribly deformed nose. "I have ruined my whole future with my nose" was the leitmotif. It sounded as if a death sentence had already been pronounced. His willingness to see a psychiatrist was perhaps the expression of a slender, desperate hope to have this sentence commuted at the last moment. Florian's nose looked completely inconspicuous to me.

His arguments were full of reproach, but also of self-blame: "What have I done to myself?" and "I have exiled myself". These statements called to mind the well-known adolescent fear of having damaged oneself by masturbating.

With regard to the family situation, there was an extensive family history of schizophrenia. Florian's father was an artist, a sensitive man, who showed much interest in his son and tried very hard to identify with his suffering, his interests, but who in this identification—as in his other relationships—came very close to his *vis-à-vis*, in a somewhat feminine way. Florian's mother was also difficult to pin down. She had a long history of anorexia nervosa, a cool objectivity, and an odd distance. Only in crisis situations did the "unrelatedness" in her relationships, also the lack of logical consequence in her sentences, become apparent. In the middle of the therapy, she left the family rather abruptly, with an ease that was unusual in her social setting.

In Florian's past history, which I cannot go into here, there are many symptoms that indicate that the early tuning-in between the anorexic mother and Florian did not run an optimum course.

As an infant he was "always angry" and spat up a great deal. Between meals he cried long and loudly, but when nursing he was very slow. Florian's mother speaks of this time in terms that reflect an astonished, respectful distance from her son. Only much later during therapeutic identification do I see an image of the other side of the dyadic mirror: I imagine an infant who desperately searches for "holding" because he lacks the strength and the ability to hold himself together and who longs for a mirroring close at hand; he cannot get enough of such a mirroring as he has difficulty introjecting this image; this mirroring, as we know (Winnicott, 1967), enables the child to experience himself as a whole.

Of course such a reconstruction, which is primarily represented as an image in the psychotherapist's fantasy, is an attempt to make sense of the situation, experienced at the interface of transference and countertransference. These experiences are often inexpressible or at least difficult to verbalize. I think that these fantasized reconstructions permit—although hermeneutically dubious—a kind of triangulation between the patient, myself, and the "construct", which, according to my experience, in turn promotes therapeutic "reverie": the ability to take up and to contain projections and to give them back in some structured form. But they are definitely not the material for "genetic interpretations".

> [This] analytic situation built up in my mind a sense of witnessing an extremely early scene. I felt that the patient had witnessed in infancy a mother who dutifully responded to the infant's emotional displays. The dutiful response had in it an element of impatient "I don't know what's the matter with the child." My deduction was, that in order to understand what the child wanted the mother should have treated the infant's cry as more than a demand for her presence. From the infant's point of view she should have taken into her, and thus experienced, the fear that the child was dying. It was this fear that the child could not contain. . . . An understanding mother is able to experience the feeling of dread that this baby was striving to deal with by projective identification, and yet retain a balanced outlook. This patient had to deal with a mother who could not tolerate experiencing such feelings and rejected . . . by denying them ingress. To some this reconstruction will appear unduly fanciful; to me it does not seem forced. [Bion, 1959, pp. 103–104]

Bion does, however, write in the same essay:

> I must refer to *inborn characteristics* and the part they play in producing attacks by the [psychotic] infant on all that links him to the breast, namely, primary aggression and envy. The seriousness of these attacks is enhanced if the mother displays the kind of unreceptiveness which I have described. [p. 105]

At this point, we should differentiate between the concepts *holding, containing,* and *reverie,* which are often used in treating the severely ill as if such terms were synonymous. I refer to them again and again in this chapter. Winnicott's famous "mirror" concept states that the mother's face is an emotional mirror of the infant's and toddler's. Through this mirror the child experiences its inner state. Winnicott's view is closely related to the Kleinian "introjective–projective cycles", but this visual interaction concerns a later period of development. This interaction can only be disrupted by the external object. "Whereas Winnicott's 'holding' is to support the infant's unwavering belief in his own omnipotence", Bion's concept of "reverie" lies in the "mother's willingness to provide a container function for understanding the infant's reality, in order to support his loss of omnipotence" (Hinshelwood, 1989, pp. 420–421). It very much presupposes a "third" in the mind of the mother (Green). Segal provides a precise description of "containing":

> When an infant has an intolerable anxiety, he deals with it by projecting it into the mother. The mother's response is to acknowledge the anxiety and do whatever is necessary to relieve the infant's distress. The infant's perception is that he has projected something intolerable into his object, but the object was capable of containing it and dealing with it. He can then reintroject . . . an anxiety modified by having it contained. He also introjects an object capable of containing and dealing with anxiety. The containment of anxiety by an external object capable of understanding is the beginning of mental stability. This mental stability may be disrupted by two sources. The mother may be unable to bear the infants projected anxiety. . . . It may also be disrupted by excessive destructive omnipotence of the infant's fantasy. *In this model the analytic situation provides the container.* [Segal, 1975, pp. 134–135, emphasis added]

In fact, the understanding and the therapeutic epistemophilia—that is, the willingness to accept the projection of the patient and to make it understandable and bearable for him in this way—is at the centre of the modern Kleinian technique.

* * *

Florian, said his parents, "was not defiant but only coercive". This "coercion" consisted in insistence on having objects such as nails, screwdrivers, and so on, which he needed for his early technical abilities and interests. "He always wanted to do things which were more appropriate for a child about three years older: he would hopelessly overtax himself and always end up despairing. As a 3-year-old, he was occupied with his father's tools. He was not able to play with toy surrogates." He was also unacquainted with role-play or the "what-if" symbolic games of children.

I asked myself what significance these circumstances might have for Florian's pathology. We know that, for one thing, schizophrenia is a disruption in the process of symbolization and desymbolization. We know very little about the anamnesis of such disturbances in child play development, unless we want to accept without question Kleinian research about children's psychoses as the anamnesis of adolescent psychoses. Interestingly, American research on homosexuality does contain such research material. Siegel showed that none of her homosexual patients had ever played with dolls or animals or played the usual role-plays (Dorpat, 1990, p. 123).

As far as I know, Melanie Klein was the first to demonstrate that in children's psychosis substitutive symbol formation is disrupted and this disruption is analogous to that experienced by schizophrenics. Segal discusses this most eloquently in "Notes on Symbol Formation" (1957).

The Winnicottian concept provides another perspective: one could also ask what the significance was in the adolescent pathology, and particularly in psychotic transference, of this early inability to play. Winnicott sees a direct line from transitory phenomena to play, from individual play to group play and, further, to social experiences and to social competence in distinguishing between closeness and distance: "When one witnesses an infant's employment of a transitional object, the first not-me possession, we are witnessing *both the child's first use of a symbol and the first experience of play*" (Winnicott, 1971, emphasis added).

The lack of an intermediate space is almost a tangible countertransference experience in relationships with patients like Florian. There is often no middle ground between boundless, devouring closeness and astronomical distance. If the analyst succeeds in establishing the first common symbols with the patient often through play, psychic growth may follow.

We do not learn anything about oedipal interests while listening to the parents.

Only latency will be idealized by Florian. With his intelligence and his technical gifts, the lonely, eccentric boy was able to develop a sort of autarch omnipotence. Puberty, with all its painful dependencies, meant facing the loss of this narcissistic heaven.

The crisis began subtly: at about the age of 14, Florian became increasingly morose, withdrew even further, spent a lot of time unhappy, lying in bed. After many years of therapy, Florian gave me a plausible description of what had triggered his breakdown: after a few rendezvous with a girl about his age—which of course required a lot of courage on his part—she dropped him. "I was smashed to pieces", he later said appropriately. Years later it became apparent that this narcissistic destruction in an initial sexual dependence had become equivalent to existential destruction.

Beginning of therapy

In the end, we never really know what enables us to establish rapport with some—certainly not all—patients during the first therapy session, no matter how closed up they seem to be.

One might think that it often happens through eye contact. However, this was not true of Florian—in the first years he never looked at me. He would come in with his eyes lowered, his shoulders somewhat hunched; he would put his backpack down beside him, press his lips together and with a small sigh drop into the chair. Then, he would say he was not doing well; he could not go on like this; something had to happen. He came three times a week for 50 minutes.

I felt pressured. His suffering was threatening. I gave him psychopharmaca. This did not help, but it gave us both the feeling that we were doing something. We could try out the effects of the drugs "together", determining how to adapt the dosage "together". It was as if Florian took the tablet every night as a kind of transitional object. Also, these drugs helped me to control my own anxiety about a suicidal youth.

In the first weeks my verbal interventions were tentative. Whenever he returned to the subject of his nose as the source of his unhappiness, I said that perhaps the dissatisfaction with his nose came from a deeper dissatisfaction with himself. This was a very tangential approach to his problems. During this period, I spent a lot of time thinking about sexuality; the connection between pubertal development, masturbation, and problems of phallicity seemed so obvious. The frugality of his communications, his emphasis on being a "perfectionist and an aesthete", and the function of the nose as an olfactory organ could also point to anal-sadistic fantasies. But my cautious attempts to talk about the disturbing aspects of sexuality were coldly dismissed. I did not insist on such interventions, but I let him see that this was out of respect for him and that I continued to have my own ideas. Only many years later did I realize how precisely he had been able to lead me, so that I did not know or say too little or too much.

How much control we allow a patient to have over our interpretation practices is a question of therapeutic style. We are concerned here with the patient's tolerance for "difference", for "separateness". There may be good reasons for interpreting this control and tyrannical intolerance at the outset. However, the process of mourning over the condition that the other is another may be the final goal of a psychosis therapy, not its beginning. This view, of course, marks in terms of technique the choice of a certain track between technical alternatives.

Further technical alternatives will present themselves to every psychoanalyst who tries to integrate with Kleinian or other techniques her fundamental understanding of the psychodynamics of adolescence as taught by Laufer and Laufer (1984). As is well known, the Laufers' thinking about the psychopathology of adolescence centres on the adolescent's pathological-defensive approach to the reality of his new sexually mature body. Consequently, they see the aim of every pathology as the destruction of the adolescent's own, new sexuality, in the hope of being able to sustain a non-sexual, non-incestuous self. Their interpretations are thus targeted at this sexuality that drives the adolescents "crazy". Though I owe the Laufers a debt of gratitude for great parts of my understanding of the psychodynamics of adolescent breakdown, I have come to the conclusion that if psychotic young people consistently refuse "sexual interpretations", I must see this rejection as more than just resistance: they just cannot deal with such interpretations, because they frequently cannot experience any interpretation as interpretation. They experience it as an attack on a highly vulnerable, fragmented self which is barely kept together by a bizarre image of their body. To my mind, only after having dealt with the very pathological defences as they appear in the transference (all forms of denial of dependence, splitting, projective identification, confusion, defensive fragmentation, etc.) is the very ill adolescent capable of understanding productively so called sexual interpretations.

* * *

The way that Florian dealt with his bottomless depression seemed just as important. In answer to his statement, "My life is ruined, I no longer have any hope", I could only answer: "Perhaps right now your hope appears to be deposited with me; while you do not feel it, I may feel it."

With this, of course, a projective identification is addressed: simultaneously it is an early offer, an invitation on the part of the analyst, to conceive all sorts of projections, to share bits and pieces of the fragmented patient. Note the double meaning of the word "conceive". But, we should be aware at the same time that with this "hope" a "good part" is being split off into the analyst. This projection must therefore be made comprehensible to the patient (he must be given a receipt for his deposit in me), otherwise it would mean a depletion, an impoverishment of the patient's self.

The first dream

After two months, Florian had the first dream which in its manifest text is as short as most of his subsequent ones: *"In a pit. I was at the edge of the pit, there was very little water in the pit. I sat down, I fished something out. With a stick, I moved the water. I thought it was disgusting . . . looked for something in it. But, it was like a cess-pit."*

My own idea was that the cesspool, fishing rod, and disgusting water were related to his masturbation. But since Florian would dismiss such interpretations, I tried to stick to the patient's symbol language and said that I thought he experienced the "disgusting matter" as a product of himself but it also contained an element of hope for him. When I was listening to the dream, I could see a treasure, a piece of gold or perhaps a gold ring, that he was trying to fish out of the disgusting pit; that perhaps it was precisely in the disgusting that the valuable was hidden. But his obsession with his nose kept him from directly confronting what he experienced as his disgusting product.

I still find this dream and both of our associations with it to be the basis for everything that happened afterwards. We somehow made a pact at this moment. For the first time, I succeeded in sharing the hope that had previously been deposited with me and in showing him that it was an expression of his own hope (projected into me). And that hope—the golden treasure—was precisely in the disgusting—that is, in sexuality, perhaps even in the "dirty" pregenital sexuality—and that I, for my part, was not afraid of it and even saw something golden in it.

My use of gold corresponds to Benedetti's concept of "positivizing" (1983). In a personal communication, he said: "From the willingness of the therapist to bring into discussions with the patient intense counter-images that originate in the therapeutic fantasy through identifying with the patient's suffering . . . these therapeutic ideas run counter to the gloomy images of the patient's experiences, do not want to be contradicted by the psychopathology." Amazingly, Florian assimilated this image, for years later he spoke of "his dream with the golden treasure".

My interpretation also expressed my first working hypothesis: "As long as you are obsessed with your nose, you do not have to confront more frightening matters." After this dream our relationship deepened. I was able to address the hypothesis of *the nose as defence* as a hypothesis of resistance: "As long as you only talk to me about your nose, we cannot talk about anything else together. You exclude me." For months, this interpretation, *nose as resistance,* became the refrain of my attempts to understand our communication. After giving me a taste of understanding, Florian usually treated me as "psychosomatics" treat their doctors: he let me feel his very deep suffering, so that I felt completely helpless, but all attempts on my part to "understand", to get in touch with, this suffering came up against an icy, sometimes ironic dismissal: "That is just psycho-stuff. . . . My only problem is my nose."

Yet accounts also appeared of a desolate, dead, chaotic inner world, of a mute anger: rotten trees, mouldy cheese, bare trees, wolves, dead forests were the recurring subjects of his dreams. They led me to see how chaotic, how fragmentary, his inner world seemed to him.

In transference, he could only show his aggressiveness *ex negativo*, in his tortuous, sometimes terrible silences, in the meagreness of his dreams, by rejecting my attempts to comment on his dreams—that is, in the silent put-down of my efforts. With all my sympathy for him, I had to be careful not to let him force me into a masochistic position. It helped tremendously that besides his appalling moroseness, Florian was able to hang onto a very thin strand of humour at this time.

During this period, his parents separated. From then on, Florian was living in the empty house with his father, who looked after him "like a mother", while his mother distanced herself even further from him.

At about this time, I began to notice that in his sexual confusion Florian began to ruffle my sexual identity towards him. Or, rather, the other way around: as a reflection of my uncertain sexual identity in countertransference, I could sense something of his confusion. Despite his "orphaned" condition, he did not make me feel very "motherly", and even less "feminine". When, in phantasy I tried to mobilize such feelings, I was afraid that I would ruin something. But, I also did not feel at all masculine; rather, more like something asexual, professional, wearing an imagined doctor's white coat. This appeared probably the least dangerous course for Florian. I now think that this asexual countertransference "in a white coat" corresponded to the heaven of the pre-pubertal bisexual omnipotence, an escape from Florian's later desires. It corresponded to Florian's effort to deny the reality of his sexually mature body. And, again, I felt that I had no choice but to collude with this defence. It took a lot of "tuning in" before I was able to move freely in this relationship. I fully agree with Searles (1965) that in the psychotherapy of psychoses the integrative work begins at the edges of the personality, starting from the outside, with the integrative efforts of the person who has to provide countertransference. I would like to re-emphasize, though, that based on other technical concepts (e.g. the Laufers'), one could have legitimately proceeded in an entirely different fashion.

Or, in the strict Kleinian tradition, for example, my countertransference could rightly be viewed as a sterilized expression of a very intrusive, compelling projection of a deeply frightening unconscious fantasy of the "combined parent figure" (i.e. a fusion of the motherly and fatherly part-objects, or rather a mother with a father inside her) and would be the occasion perhaps for direct interpretation (Klein, 1923).

The delusion of being poisoned

At the beginning of the third year of therapy, upon my return from summer vacation, an emergency telephone call from Florian's father awaited me: Florian was completely chaotic, he was sitting amidst torn-up newspapers, trembling and despairing, he was worried about gases and environmental pollution. Florian wanted to come to see me immediately.

He had now developed a delusion of being poisoned. He had read in the newspaper about environmental pollution through formaldehyde, which was also contained in plastic panels. His father, an interior decorator, had many pavatex panels in his studio. Florian was deathly afraid. He felt the odour pouring in through the cracks around the door and had to keep airing the house. It was penetrating him through all his pores. This delusion was first focused on his father's pavatex panels, then expanded to all kinds of pollutants. It made life with Florian extremely trying.

In this difficult period, therapy became tremendously lively. Earlier, Florian and his thoughts were hermetically sealed in his nose problems. With the delusion of being poisoned, his anxieties opened up into the interpersonal. The world came in with the odours, and in therapy, too, a door opened. It seemed to me that this new type of delusion—although it may appear "pathological"—meant progress: the patient ventured out into the interpersonal field—that is, into the field of dependencies.

I first tried to address his environmental awareness, his openness to external influences, and his sensitivity to them (cf. Benedetti, 1983). It meant a slight narcissistic upgrading of Florian, who saw himself as completely helpless at this time. On the other hand, to a psychotic patient such a therapeutic reply has an integrating function for the patient, since he is reflected; it is he who opens himself up to the external world.

In a second step, I tried to locate the source of these permeating odours, and it was clear that they were related to his father; it was he who flowed through the cracks around the door and penetrated into his pores. It was not easy to live in this two-man household and break away from each other as would usually be the case at this age. Without using the word "homosexuality", we managed to work through not only much of Florian's fear of fatherly penetration, but also his ambivalence towards his father: besides interpreting his anger at his father, we were also able to explain his longing for him, which was evident in his inability to forget about him even when he was not present. Analogies to the "Schreber case" (Freud, 1911c [1910]) are obvious.

At a deeper level, there was Florian's feeling of persecution by a poisonous "breast", which he experienced and had to enact dramatically—as befitted the confused gender relationships in this family—in the symbiosis with his father. The fact that this representation could cause his ego boundaries to collapse in such a destructive way also appeared related to my holiday. In the symbiotic relationship father–Florian, I probably played the "third", who helps ease dependence (in this case experienced as toxic) on the mother-figure.

* * *

Once that had been worked through, and Florian was making educational and social progress in the outside world (as I learned only indirectly), more than six months of darkness followed in therapy. It was like a boat trip in the November fog. I felt as if I had been absorbed into his dark inner world. I often had no new ideas. It seemed to me as if only a shared suffering existed. Gradually, I contented myself with the fact that he did not commit suicide, cut off his nose, or stop therapy. Now I think that this "winter"—it really was winter—this seeing it through together, was necessary to enable the subsequent breakthrough. The closeness that arose in this way, his absorption of my person into his life, later gave the therapy the power for change.

As a counter-movement, however, I had to answer for external reality. For example, I once thought of examining his nose like "a real doctor". I knew that at this time he was often studying himself in the mirror, which is a typical dysmorphophobic ritual and is also the ritual of many schizophrenics, like the amazed way they gaze at their hands.

I asked him if I could examine his nose more closely. He moved his chair to the window, I put on my glasses, and we were, without my having the slightest feeling of disrupting the setting, "nose to nose". I was quasi taking inventory of his individual blackheads, dandruff, etc. I thought that he was listening intently. In fact, as I learned later, he was studying *my* nose, counting my blackheads. Afterwards, he seemed very relaxed, and I had the impression that something had happened. I thought it was the seriousness with which after the inspection I said, in our shared tone, "Florian, I think you are a little bit crazy", which led to the temporary relaxation. That and my smiling "excuse me" certainly played some role. Years later, he told me that this scene confirmed his suspicion that I too had a "weird" nose, that I was a person like he. He often said later: "Everything that happened between us would not have been possible if you had had a perfect nose." The mirror thus came alive.

The therapeutic effectiveness of this scene, so unimaginable with neurotic patients, can be explained on many levels. Florian was able to expand, to project, his imagined defect in the sense of a more or less delusional mirror transference to my nose. Hence, he was no longer alone with his nose, the hallmark of his autism. At the same time, however, by accepting my nose as a "co-nose", he was able to introject a piece of my favourable relationship to my own nose, which though not especially beautiful, was at least not what I considered ugly. My saying to him as from my inmost self, "Florian, you are a little bit crazy", and his acceptance of such a statement in an amused fashion made him able to feel a part of my (i.e. external) reality, which at the same time was part of our shared symbiotic shell (the November days). I owe this interpretation of the dynamics of this session to Florian, who later tried very hard to understand "his earlier nose delusion", and to explain it to me. Two years later, when his first girlfriend heard what was by then the "old nose story", she shook her head and said, "You're crazy", which made him laugh out loud. He thought he had finally overcome his "nose".

The fear of dissolving

Now, with a certain logic, the next delusion began: "I'm dissolving", "I'm no longer in one piece", "The landscape, too, is falling apart", "The worst part is that my inner landscape sometimes falls apart." When I tried to show him that perhaps holding on to his nose had helped him to protect himself against the falling apart that he now felt, he said in a diffuse delusional mood:

> "Now everything is different: now I cannot bear the inner, yes *inner image* of my nose. Like a persecution complex from my own nose, don't you see, and then my surroundings are nothing. Or I am nothing in my surroundings because I am dissolving from shame and unbearableness. When I am with a crowd of people, I can hardly stand the torture. I have to dissolve so that I am not defenceless in the crowd, so that I am not trampled. I am just about to lose my mind. Then when it gets bad, I destroy something so that I do not go crazy."

It was clear: as he described this to me, at the moment of communication, he was able to "defragment" himself, he was no longer really "psychotic". He spoke from the vantage point of the observing ego over alienation and fragmentation experiences. But he was only able to do so contained in the matrix of the actual therapeutic communication, sitting face to face with the therapist. When he was alone, he fell apart psychotically, and the internalized image of therapy apparently offered no help. On the contrary, his nose, which without therapy functioned as a keystone holding together the wobbly vault of the ego, crashed into the vault because of therapy; it was now experienced as an "inner persecutor" and threatened further to fragment his barely assembled system—his fragile ego. The passage quoted above beautifully illustrates how his images of being persecuted abruptly alternated between inside (through his "nose") and outside (being trampled by the crowd) and thus attacked his ability to reason. "I was just about to lose my mind."

This point also seems significant as an illustration of the fact that dysmorphophobic patients, as various authors have noted, often decompensate psychotically following an operation that they had insisted on. A similar situation had now arisen with Florian: "the nose symptom" had been amputated, but the crucial difference was that psychotic regression within the matrix of therapeutic regression was able to be answered and processed.

Two years later, looking back on this crisis, Florian explained:

> "Now my personality seems like a landscape where I can go walking. At that time, such an idea would never have occurred to me. It was only a threat. A battlefield. Jumping from one endangered spot to another. My thoughts were focused on what was threatening me, and I wasn't even able to ask what it actually was that was threatened. You were the only one to ask, to ask about my substance; without this I would have completely forgotten that I had such a substance. Once you told me that my hope was deposited with you or something like that. That sounds quite nice, but more important is the *knowledge of the sheer existence of such substance,* that at least you were able to perceive it. That is the structure of hope."

It was also impressive how this period of dissolving experiences went hand in hand with openly articulated anaclitic wishes: extra hours were requested, and telephone calls during his vacation often took place at this time. Usually I went along with these wishes and did not interpret them. This is a decision as to technique: patients with questionable symbolization skills often experience an interpretation of anaclitic wishes as a rejection; they often withdraw because they cannot deal with the insight into their dependency, which they experience as "total", or with the elemental rage that this releases. That could not be my goal. A non-interpretation, on the other hand, also sets a course: *the patient can experience it as an invitation to settle, to nest further into the frame of the therapy and thus within the confines, the frame, of the therapist herself.* This was, as I later found out, the case for Florian. At this time, by the end of the session, his depersonalization experiences were usually mitigated, the delusional mood gone. Of course, later we would have to pay for so much dependency.

At about this time, he also passed his final high-school examinations and began his university studies. It once again became clear how a regression in therapy was connected with a kind of "progression" in his "external life". Precisely during this period of "dissolving", he was able to "loosen" his relationship armour *vis-à-vis* real objects: peers of both sexes, with whom he associated for the first time, went on holiday, and so forth.

At this time, I was also able to learn something about how Florian experienced this feeling of dissolution in situations involving human relationships. For example, he talked to colleagues and then said:

> "I feel rejected by the person I'm talking to, not by the real person, he doesn't notice anything, because a pseudo-part of me continues to take part in the conversation, while I disappear inside myself. The true part of me is dead, invisible. I feel myself disappearing, the cold dissolving, and that's horrible. A normal person cannot imagine how it feels."

An expression of transference is contained in this "a normal person can . . ."—that is, "You, normal person, can't understand me now, I disappear from view." I tried to tell him that this disappearing does not "happen", he does it to himself while talking to someone. He disappears under a magic hood: "Hocus-pocus, now you have to look for Florian." His somewhat arch, suddenly warmer expression indicated that this time I was not on the wrong track, and I tried to work out with him what was behind this urge to hide, dissolve, not let himself be touched. Perhaps, that we should look for him and hold him? "No, not at all. I think that what is behind this is hate."

It was the first verbalized, uncoded message of an archaic, diffuse feeling of hate towards a hostile environment, which overwhelms him especially when he comes closer to people and that he tries to defend himself against by "dissolving", "disappearing", fragmenting—fragmentation as psychotic defence.

"And the hate—between the two of us?" I asked, to which he replied: "It is as if I had put chaos in a little box on the table between us and we were gazing at this box together without knowing exactly what was in it."

This sentence demonstrates that when hate was discussed in transference, the patient cleverly presented it, for the time being, in a toy box with secret contents, a kind of Pandora's box. But the patient was also making an offer—to "dig" into this matter together. It is clear that a psychoanalytic breakthrough could only be obtained once this box with its terrible contents would also fly open in transference and the patient's deep hate would touch me with its force and thus could be processed. But that would take time. Much later we were to understand that Pandora's box at a deeper level is not on the table, but projected into my body. Theoretically, from a Kleinian point of view, this could have been inferred at this stage. My technique forbids me to interpret such ideas prior to a shared emotional experience with the patient.

In another example from this period, Florian says:

> "It is as if I were in a pool where one or the other plug is outside and I swim around under water and try to close it. Again I cannot find any connection with my surroundings. . . . Fear sits deep within me . . . I am at everyone's mercy, I feel like I am full of holes . . ."

Although this sentence sounds metaphorical because of the "like", in its context it is a concretizing, schizophrenic statement expressing the lack of structure and boundaries, the whole existential tragedy of self-perception. In such moments, for reasons not clear to me but nevertheless imperative, I was unable to address his paranoid hatred in transference, which can, for example, be heard in the sentence "I am at everyone's mercy". I could only say: "It seems to me, that we two are trying hard to build a basin, where you yourself can push in and pull out the plug." I had to ask myself, if I was "turning a blind eye" on his hate. I knew very well that this may be the contents of his uncontained pool. Nevertheless, I chose addressing rather the predicament of fragmentation than the forces that lead to it.

This corresponds to a therapeutic approach that I had learned from Benedetti (1983):

> In the psychotherapy of psychosis, it is rarely possible to take away a patient's symptom solely with the help of an interpretation, even if it is repeated over and over. Frequently, we find that the symptom only disappears when the therapist can communicate with the patient within the symptom, i.e. within the security boundaries which the symptom demands. [p. 73]

According to Medri (1983):

> the schizophrenic pathology . . . (can) largely be traced back to a fragmentation of the ego, as the neurotic to a conflict situation, the therapeutic answer looks different than in classic psychoanalysis and has other goals; . . . not to reveal what is repressed, but rather to communicate the form and structure which are missing. On the other hand, the psychopathology of the id is based on a massive narcissistic emptiness, which cannot be filled up using a simple technical operation. [p. 81]

As mentioned earlier, the Kleinian tradition provides a sharp contrast. According to modern Kleinian views, which I basically share, primitive hate and envy on the one hand and fragmentation, projection, and so forth on the other are part and parcel of the same pathology. In this opinion, this "emptiness" is filled up in such a way that the projections are enriched and "improved" by the therapist's understanding and making-sense-of interpretations. That cannot be called a "simple technical operation". The key question, however, remains as to which "return"—that is, interpretation—the patient will perceive as enrichment, "filling", and which as rejection, as unchanged—that is, toxic counter-projection. I frequently feel that interpreting or even alluding to latent transference hate makes psychotic patients, with their deficient symbolization, at times feel as if they were rejected and attacked. "Building a basin" means also building a common symbolic language as a transitional space that connects and protectively separates us at the same time.

The first delusional transference

Florian increasingly complained about a burning at the back of his head, making him feel as though he were completely "closed". At the same time, he suffered from hypochondriac delusions related to his eyes: he could no longer see properly. What was he trying not to see? This happened at a time when he was involved in more intense, more erotic human relationships, with what was for him an astonishing boldness. He had fallen in love. I felt that secret thoughts, which he had to kill, were burning at the back of his mind. Or, that like a marmot awakening in the spring, he had to squint, blink his eyes, if he were going to allow the light of the world—including the world of desires—to come in. (As Freud pointed out, the schizophrenic tends to feel that his surface is full of innumerable holes. The other "holes", eyes, ears, etc. are therefore often highly cathected.) That he himself noticed that he was "closed" was progress to the extent that he noted the relational aspect of this physical symptom, rather than in the case of "his nose", which was alienated from him as a "bizarre object".

We had scarcely brought this into the open when Florian began cautiously to allude to, then became more and more reproachful about, the drugs prescribed early in therapy, which could have been what had ruined the back of his head. Of course, I was the one who had given him the drugs years ago (and in a sense what was at the back of his mind, too). It was not difficult to relate these fears that I had poisoned him with "my" drugs to his fear of being poisoned by his father's pavatex panels. He still remembered how much object-relation anxiety was packed into his fear of being poisoned. And so, for the first time during therapy, we had arrived at a delusional transference. The valves were opened, and his strongest reproaches, which at first often seemed very chaotic and contradictory, were directed at me: the drugs were, as he said, poisonous because they forced their way inside him; but they were also terrible because they were creating a distance between us. This touches upon the basic schizophrenic object-relation dilemma. I gave him drugs instead of giving him myself, as a way of getting rid of him, of keeping him at a distance emotionally, but it was also the action of a witch exercising her power. The delusion that, if I wanted to, I could cure him in a flash was expressed repeatedly; but supposedly I didn't want to help him, I wanted to destroy him.

During these hours, I felt very afraid; the psychosis, which had first been closely packed in his "nose", was suddenly between us and I understood very little. I also had to ask myself whether an earlier, systematic interpretation of his initially unconscious hate in transference would have prevented such a development. That may well have been the case. Now, though, I am firmly convinced that the treatment of schizophrenics cannot be aimed at preventing a delusional transference; on the contrary, the psychotherapist's offer of a relationship is optimum when the drama of the "introjective–projective cycle" (Volkan, 1976) can be experienced in the therapeutic encounter.

The counterpart of the projection–introjection drama, as is so clear in this passage (the patient forces his hate into me by projection, it forces itself back into him in his fantasy as poison, etc.), is the typical schizophrenic coupling of the object-hunger and the object-anxiety, which is no less noticeable. Considered in this way, Florian's reproaches were not as "illogical" as they sounded.

What impressed me most was the strong, archaic-like wish that I could deliver him from his tribulations—his being "closed", his being ruined, the aching in the back of his head—with one stroke, and at the same time his equally enormous fear of the witch's power, of the "giant mother" who would actually be able to save him. I felt it important not to explain the absurd incompatibility of these needs but, rather, the tragedy of their belonging together, which we often suspect as the source of psychotic disturbances: it is the wish for an omnipotent self-object that would be able to protect one from all of one's inner persecutors—that is, from bottomless hate and its consequences and at the same time the paranoid fear of its destructiveness. The patient was afraid of everything in the transference: it sometimes seemed that in such hours I meant only destruction and betrayal to the patient. But still he managed not to kill my belief that all this made sense. Once after one of these hours I found myself mumbling to myself: "and the good object is still not dead". I must have had my doubts.

Melting

It would be naive to think that all we need to do is name those impulses that fragment time, the body, and the representation of self and object and then these schizophrenic symptoms will disappear. Instead, I think, as do Searles, Benedetti, and so on, that the integrative work has to take place in the therapist's psyche first. Florian knew very well that I experienced him, his body, his bizarre world of thoughts, his and our time together, as a whole and that I was able to take up and reflect the hate that he had directed against me, without shattering our relationship (our "linking") and in particular my whole image of him. He gradually succeeded in introjecting some of my view (i.e. of a whole Florian) not because I said anything very clever during this period, but because I was quiet and close to him. Searles and Benedetti speak of a "therapeutic symbiosis". An example of a sign of such a "symbiosis" (in the broadest sense of the word) was Florian's foot, which, like my own, would almost regularly "fall asleep" towards the end of the session (something that has hardly ever happened to me with any other patient). The fact that both of us often stood up limping and stiff played a comparable role now for Florian as my "similar" nose had earlier.

Searles's (1965) comments on such experiences provide a good illustration of my point of view:

> ... one of the major functions of this (therapeutic) symbiosis is, in my experience, that it enables the patient's increasing integration to occur as it were external to himself. Mystical though it sounds, it is based upon logically understandable clinical phenomena.
>
> ... Once the relationship has progressed far enough, once to put it another way, the patient's integration has succeeded far enough, for the therapist to achieve such an integrated inner picture of the patient, from then on he inevitably responds to the patient in this vein, namely as a person, and in accordance with long known theories of the development of the self, the patient, in finding himself persistently so responded to by the therapist ... comes to such an image of himself at an unconscious as well as a conscious level. [pp. 308–309]

During the course of this development, a closeness arose between us that was different to that of the shapeless November days. It was a closeness of common understanding, the epistemophily: a period of differentiated transference insights on the great and problematical closeness to me, or part-aspects of me, began.

The rediscovered gift of symbolic thinking, the "as if", was also noteworthy: "When I am far away from you, then I am far away from me." In one of his dreams, *a part of him stood with a part of me at his grave and we cried together*—a part of him was buried. Or such dialogues as follows developed:

F: "Now I do not feel any hate towards you: You are too close for me to feel hate; at most I have put you with my worst ego—that is, beyond hate."

JP: "As if I were a part of you?"

F: "In a way, yes. Sometimes you are another person,. At other times you are so close to me that I cannot have any specific feeling about you." [There the narcissistic emptiness spills over into the object.] "That is why in such moments it is so important for me not to have to think that you have failed; then I would not have any chance, I would fall. But, if you are someone else then the competitive situation arises, the rage, then the melting, and then total emptiness and timelessness. When I finally no longer fall apart physically, then time falls apart on me. I simply do not experience it."

This passage is impressive because it shows how a healthy part of the patient can speak spontaneously and with deep insight about the torment that accompanies the elementary differentiation between self and object in general and in transference in particular. Furthermore, it offers insight on the relationship between the most difficult self-pathology and the schizophrenic disruption of reasoning, as Bion so brilliantly described it under the concept "Attacks on Linking" (1959). In terms of therapy, what seems crucial to me is that such *disruptions of thought* can be understood and processed together in the *transference dynamics.*

Then Florian had idyllic dreams of shared drives in the car: I drive him to a lecture; my car waits for him while he puts himself in danger as a reporter, observing the events of a war in a house (surely representing the internal fighting over his sexuality with blood, women, etc.).

In the belly: the birth

When we reached this point, I thought that I "had caught sight of land" in the therapy and could communicate with a mature, healthy part of Florian; his introspection, his symbolization ability, and his ability to see himself and me as separate objects, each with our own history even within therapy, made me think about *time* in general and the time of saying "good-bye". I felt somewhat relieved.

However, my idea proved to be an illusion, and it is worth considering whether it was not precisely this countertransference—that is, my experience of a welcome separateness—that helped to trigger the following development.

Florian, somewhat stronger in his social life, the crises of a love relationship behind him, decided after much hesitation to take part in a student sports camp. The fact that he was not at all able to keep pace with his peers, the teasing, the insults, the jealousy and feelings of envy during these days became a nightmare for him and took on an overpowering role in transference. That I "had let him go" became almost the sole topic of the last year of therapy. "You should have known, told me not to go, not let me be humiliated" was the so-called "neurotic" variant of his accusation. "You wanted to throw me out of your life, leave me to nothingness, let me freeze", he continued. "You know I carry your thoughts and when your thoughts are bad, I fall apart." The boundary between self and object was once again obscured, as was the boundary between reality and fantasy: "You have carried me for years, and now . . ."

Since the word "carried" had up to now been our metaphor for the opposite of "dropping", I first understood this as symbolic until Florian explained that he meant the whole thing concretely. He was inside me. He said:

F: "You have carried me for years inside of you."

JP: "You mean in spirit?"

F: "You, with your 'spirit'! *Inside of you*. You know, every time when I could not go on, you let me live inside of you. You had to feel everything. Have you never heard of placental circulation? When I go under in . . . you feel it in your womb. If you don't you are death. And I am death. And if I seem to still be living, it's only because I have erased you and me. I only survive because I have destroyed you. You are dead and I am only hate."

"Omnipotent destructive narcissism", as Herbert Rosenfeld (1987) described it, was raging here along with the unmistakable delusion that he was very concretely in my pregnant body. "But why?", I asked myself, quite terrified. Because he no longer felt carried in the transference as he had been previously. With his increasing perception of "skin", of self and object boundaries between us, with the initial withdrawal of the projective identification, once again the existential panic arose. The omnipotent destructive narcissism is like Bick's (1968) "second skin": it protects one from "nothingness". The delusional idea of my being pregnant with him appears at first glance as an attempt to bring himself into safety near the end of therapy, analogous to the rapprochement during the child's individuation. Even so, it was quite frightening.

Rosenfeld (1971) talks about:

> . . . object relations of the psychotic patient in analysis where he maintains the belief that he is entirely living inside an object—the analyst—and behaves like a parasite using the capacities of the analyst, who is expected to function as his ego. . . . The parasitic patient relies entirely on the analyst, often making him responsible for his entire life. . . . It occurs at times when separation threatens or when jealousy or envy is violently stimulated . . . in outside life. [pp. 126, 135]

Both conditions (initial separation during analysis, and jealousy and envy outside analysis) were encountered in this moment. For the therapeutic process, the experience of the initial separation and the surfacing of depressive fears on the horizon were more important. Florian (and I probably too, with my vision of goodbye) was on the verge of breaking out of the therapeutic symbiotic cocoon (Searles, 1965). That meant that he began to form a more realistic image of himself, of me, of our partly common, partly not common, history. It also meant a gradual withdrawal of primitive idealization and of projective identification that had up to now guaranteed his idealized melting with me and thus a certain security.

In this delusional transference, Florian provided a mixture of pregnancy idyll and tremendous destructiveness of everything that we had "in common", which, for my part, I could hardly bear(!). Our work together seemed like a pile of rubble since he saw himself only as an annihilated victim of my indifference, untruthfulness, and lack of responsibility. It was my hate and my ill-will that kept him from his place in my body, that had for years led him astray. He was all recrimination, and I experienced his recriminations as monstrous. It was little consolation to read the stoical Bion's description of this sort of "parasitism" as the "chronic murder of patient and analyst" (quoted by Rosenfeld, 1971, p. 126).

How did I manage to get into this terrible "unwanted pregnancy", I asked myself in a fervid complementary countertransference, often outraged and totally drained after the session. I had to contemplate this carefully in order not to act out such feelings. My thinking yielded the insight that the "pregnancy" (like many other so-called unwanted ones) was perhaps not so unwanted. Possibly it was the final, almost absurd, and not-so-absurd consequence of the therapeutic offer to contain a patient. At first, this makes one shudder. It is as if the containing idea had become, so to speak, coagulated, concretized, in a delusion. In terms of body image, containing can mean pregnancy in a symbolic equation (Segal, 1957) for the psychotic patient and maybe even for the inner world of the analyst. My insight into this symmetry might provide the turning point of the analysis, the hope for a new beginning. When the patient and therapist meet symbolically at this "primaeval" point, it might be possible to set out on a new path towards maturity in the direction of the depressive position. This path will contain mourning of the projective identification, mourning of the melting and total oneness, mourning of the loss of the (self-) object, mourning of omnipotence. It means the realistic experience of separation and individuation (Hering, personal communication 1995).

With this insight, I was suddenly able to accept this "pregnancy". My countertransference was more in balance. (This was all the more important because if I had acted out my rejection, it would have been like a kind of psychic abortion. If I had, however subtly, acted out my own melting and pregnancy wishes, they would have been just as "deadly" for the psychic maturity and differentiation of the patient, a kind of incest experience.)

From this countertransference, I understood and interpreted the *wish* behind the delusion: the desire of all of us—if we believe

Ferenczi (1924), Grünberger (1971), and Chasseguet-Smirgel (1975, 1986)—to return to the womb, and, since the roles in the primary process are interchangeable, to "bear", to "carry", our objects. *This suggests that the analytic situation* (Stone, 1961)—*in particular, the idea of containment—could also be considered under certain conditions as a high sublimation of unconscious pregnancy fantasies by the analyst, in addition to the well-known reparation wishes.*

Psychoanalytic reality means accepting a wish while at the same time knowing that it cannot be fulfilled. Psychoanalytic abstinence means that the analyst, while mourning because she cannot fulfil the wish, goes ahead of the patient. It was perhaps my quiet recognition of our common, though differently formulated, desire which brought about the turning point—after weeks of wrestling to make progress—and opened the door to the possibility of a common mourning. Florian perceived, I think, my own mourning that I was unable to fulfil his wish. That is, as soon as the "I was in your belly" could be interpreted and answered as a wish, we were able to begin with the de-idealization of this "primal melting" (Ferenczi, 1924). We know that this is the way to the individual ego-ideal.

After reaching this turning point, we were able to move ahead relatively rapidly: Florian's destructive attacks gradually turned into criticism, which later included some forbearance.

The "slipping out of" the symbiosis allowed him a view of his own life story as a continuum: that led to a deep mourning for the lost years of his youth which he feared he would no longer be able to make up. He had and was able to consider his personal future for the first time and to see himself as a grown man. His reflections about the common years in therapy enabled him to form a realistic picture of his therapist, her age, her limits: this picture contained much irony, some dissatisfaction, and a touch of gratefulness. When he noticed that he "actually no longer needed me", depressive anxieties were triggered for the first time, with concern, guilt, and reparation wishes. It was impressive to see how the reparation wishes and their analysis in therapy contributed to a "humanization" of his relationships and to a joyful creativity in his research.

At the same time, he was able to conclude his studies, to fit into an academic hierarchy, to enter into friendships and sexual relationships, and later to marry, all of this with an astonishing sense of the "difference" and of the limits of others.

That was many years ago.

Shortly before I began writing this chapter, a young scientist tapped me gently on the shoulder as I was sitting as a guest in the professors' lounge at a foreign university. It took me more than a minute to recognize in this cheerful, well-balanced man my former patient. He has a good life.

Notes on Dysmorphophobia

History. The concept of dysmorphophobia (DMP) was defined by the Italian psychiatrist E. Morselli in 1886 and means fear of deformity (Morselli, 1886). Morselli's patients suffered from the belief that their face or a part of it was deformed. He categorized the new symptom as "rudimentary paranoia". School psychiatry today calls it "mono-symptomatic hypochondriac psychosis" (Munro, 1980).

With few exceptions, little was heard about DMP until the second analysis of the Wolf Man by Ruth Mack Brunswick (1929). Four years after his first analysis with Freud, the Wolf Man began to examine his nose for sebaceous glands. Later, after squeezing a pimple, he looked in the mirror and discovered a deep hole. At that moment, the well-known obsession with mirrors, so often mentioned in DMP literature, took hold; he began to constantly examine his nose and have doubts about the alleged failure of his doctors. But there is another striking motif in this patient's history: namely, his certainty that this condition can never be corrected—the doctors have botched the treatment (already described in the "past"). The shame about one's own defect is coupled with hatred of a projected figure, on whom one is totally dependent. For Mack Brunswick, there was no doubt that the hypochondria only served to defend against persecutory ideas. My patient lead me to the same conclusion. A key characteristic of the Wolf Man's persecution complex was his identification with his father, whom he regarded as castrated. Oddly enough, this characteristic was also central to my own patient and to our analysis, and we were only able to work through it after several years of rigid defence.

In 1967, Mara Selvini Palazzoli (at that time still influenced by Klein) explained the matter in this way:

> For the dysmorphophobic, the catastrophe has already taken place, as if the conflict and the suffering had deformed his body . . . instead of, as is actually the case, of having deformed his ego. We can define this type of relationship as an angry and passive dependence *vis-à-vis* the deformed object, which is incorporated with no way to get rid of it. . . . The surgeon becomes the persecutor of the patient, as if the sick person with his aggressive insistence on reconstructive surgery had been searching for just such an opportunity for a long time. [Selvini, 1967, p. 8; translated by J.P.]

Her work on DMP is fascinating because while she compares conditions such as anorexia, hypochondria, DMP, and depersonalization and treats them under the main aspect of introjection and projection of the "bad object", ideas from earlier family therapy (Bateson, etc.) already emerge. She is one of the first to note that many of these patients insist on cosmetic surgery, but that after such an operation their conditions regularly deteriorate. In my opinion, cross-connections with transsexuality are also self-evident.

The psychoanalyst Paul Schilder, in his now classic monograph *The Image and the Appearance of the Human Body* (1935), describes a case of DMP. Schilder's work is one of the first in psychoanalytic literature on the psychology of the body image, a representation of the body woven from unconscious internalized object relationships and which is separate from the empirically assembled body schema.

There is, of course, space for DMP in the Laufers' seminal work on adolescent breakdown:

> The anxiety the adolescent has about his sexual body may appear to be totally contained by a preoccupation with a specific aspect of his body, such as a fixed idea of needing to change some part of the body. This is a sign that the adolescent has been unable to contain the anxiety about his body; the threat of becoming overwhelmed has effected a split in his

> sexual body image so that only a part of it has to be rejected. In this way the adolescent can avoid a situation of complete deadlock despite the overwhelming anxiety that is being defended against. [Laufer & Laufer, 1984, p. 180]

As regards DMP, the Laufers assume something like an intermediate stage between "psychotic functioning" with the "ability to doubt" and the psychosis that does not have this capability:

> Some adolescents believe that they can acquire a different kind of body through certain actions or identifications, and they do not doubt that this is a possibility. The adolescent who . . . is convinced without doubt, that his ability to reach inner peace and contentment is dependent on the acquisition of a new kind of body as would be the case with those adolescents who insist that they must have their genitals removed or changed . . . would have to be considered as moving toward or as vulnerable to psychosis. With those adolescents who seek other forms of body change, . . . (e.g.) . . . in shape of nose, we have to consider the possibility of the move to psychosis in the future. [pp. 192–193]

Frequency. No figures are available. Andreasen and Nardach (1977) thinks that 2 per cent of the patients who consult a plastic surgeon for a cosmetic operation are dysmorphophobic. But we do not know how many patients consult plastic surgeons for cosmetic surgery. In any case, it is a rare phenomenon. In Russia, DMP seems to occur more frequently. Interestingly, "the nose" not only plays an important role in Gogol's eponymous comedy, but also in Russian folk theatre.

Prognosis. A look at the relevant literature yields an extremely depressing picture of what these young patients can expect from their futures. The authors often speak of an "ominous sign" and a "malignant disease". Connolly and Gipson (1978) looked at 202 people who had had a nose operation. Fifteen years after the rhinoplasty, of those who had had the operations for aesthetic reasons, 6 times more were schizophrenic and 3½ times more were neurotic than in a comparable group (those who had been operated on for surgical reasons), and all of the schizophrenic patients were so florid that none of them could live outside the clinic. (It should, however, be noted that other authors, such as Benedetti, 1964, and Selvini, 1967, found that a surgical reaction to the dysmorphophobic anxieties and desires can lead quite specifically to a psychotic disintegration of the patient. It could be then that the high number of cases ending as schizophrenics does not entirely reflect the "natural course" of the illness, but, rather, makes a strong statement about the effects of medical interventions.)

Nosology. I have no doubt that DMP signals a psychotic event. First, the symptomatology itself consists of an unshakeable, uncorrectable delusion that is used as the basis for a highly unrealistic, autistic social behaviour, which we really know only in the case of psychoses or, as the Laufers put it, on the way to psychoses. Second, the fact that a surgical involvement (i.e. an operation) regularly leads to psychotic disintegration supports the view that the symptom of DMP itself is a defence against more fatal psychotic conditions. Third, in the three dysmorphophobics I have treated so far, the predominant defence was "abnormal projective identification" (Bion, 1959, 1962a, 1962b) or "intrusive identification" (Meltzer, 1975), and these are signs of psychotic functioning, like fragmentation, confusion (Rosenfeld, 1966, 1971), and clearly disturbed symbolization. I tried to demonstrate in this case study that—in Bionian terminology—the "nose" can be recognized as a "bizarre object" *sensu strictu.*

Treatment. The use of neuroleptics yields temporary relief only. There is only scanty evidence in the literature of psychodynamically oriented therapies for this condition.

NOTES

1. All quotations from Benedetti are translated by the author.
2. It was as early as 1930, when schizophrenia was still called *démence précoce,* that Abely described his "*signe de miroir*". This theory states that before the outbreak of the psychosis, many patients who later become schizophrenic spend an endless amount of time looking in the mirror to assure themselves of their self or from the fear that they may have changed. This is related to other schizophrenic oddities; for example, how they stare at their

own hands in amazement while moving them back and forth in front of their eyes. I agree with Blankenburg (1982) that we should not only see the pathological in these symptoms, but also that they are the last, usually hopeless tentative attempts to re-integrate the alienated, the split-off, the fragmented, a kind of auto-protective process, or, "as if these organs were the last bastions against psychotic ego-disintegration" (Benedetti, 1964, p. 124).

3. Bick (1968), whose views come close to those of Klein and Winnicott, discussed the "skin function". The skin is the place of the first contact between mother and child, and its representation the boundary in which the inner space can develop. This "inner space" (i.e. the representation of "containment") is the precondition of the projection–introjection cycle. When the creation of this representation is disturbed for some reason, the skin is full of holes, the child experiences the most elemental of all fears: "falling apart" (analogous to Bion's, 1962b, "nameless dread", Pao's, 1979, "organismic panic", etc.). The "second skin", a manifestation of which may be the distorted perception of the other organs of sense, represents a primitive defence against this fear. Meltzer (1975) further developed Bick's ideas, which were based on the technique of observing infants which she had developed: that of "adhesive identification".
4. Glasser's (1979) "core complex" addresses to my mind the same dilemma in a clinically different situation: in perversions.

CHAPTER FIVE

Therapy for adolescents in detention for violent crime

Arnaldo Novelletto & Gianluigi Monniello

The psychotherapeutic treatment of adolescents detained for violent crimes may be based on psychoanalytic theory and technique, but it obviously cannot be called psychoanalytical treatment proper. For one thing, it is carried out in a highly peculiar setting: a juvenile prison. Our experiences can be related to those of Balier (1985) at Varces Prison in France and of Williams (1983) at Wormwood Scrubs in the United Kingdom.

This chapter springs from clinical consulting performed by both authors, at different times, for the Rome Children's Court and from exchanges of views that ensued. The hypothesis that led us to offer this contribution is that there are substantial links between certain crimes of violence committed by adolescents who cannot be considered as clinically psychotic and a mode of psychic functioning that powerfully evokes the concept of breakdown.

Frequently, we find, this psychic functioning is decisive in the genesis of the crime but is not such as to preclude or seriously impair the subject's possession of his mental faculties, which under Italian law is the condition for the penal indictment of adults (aged 18 and over).

However, the aims of this chapter do not involve forensic medicine as such. Rather, we are interested in finding the best way to provide psychological assistance to adolescents charged with or guilty of serious violent crime (murder, attempted murder, infanticide, assault for purposes of robbery or rape, etc.) both before the trial and after sentencing. Actually, we find that the judicial process in which the adolescent is caught up may offer opportunities for change and growth. If appropriately seized on by an expert adolescent therapist, these occasions can be helpful to the subject's future psychic maturation quite independently of developments on the penal and juridical front.

We describe below the cases of two boys. In the first, therapy was conducted for about six months during the period of pre-trial detention. In the second, therapy lasted for about a year and a half.

Mario

From what he told the judge, it seems that one day "Mario" (17½ years old) went to see a football game. At the entrance to the stadium, together with some other boys, he started touting his ticket to passers-by (a common practice in Italy). One of the other boys was Antonio, a former schoolmate. The two received a banknote from a passer-by and should have shared it, but Mario refused and, after getting his share of the rest, told Antonio to go away. A fight began, but the other boys broke it up. When they separated, Mario warned Antonio that he would "fix him later".

Mario attended the game, and nothing else happened. The next day he stayed at home with his mother: "I joked around with her, like I hadn't done for a long time." Then in the afternoon, without telling anybody, he took his father's hunting knife, went to Antonio's house, and asked him to come down and have a talk. Antonio came with his younger brother, and Mario had a friend of his own with him. The two started to talk but soon started fighting. Mario took a hard punch on the ear and got so angry "I no longer knew what I was doing". He pulled out the knife and stabbed Antonio several times; luckily the wounds were not too serious.

When he realized that he had blood on his hands, he broke off fighting and ran away, waving the knife in the air. Witnesses say he was screaming "I'll kill you all! I swear on my mother's dead body that I'll kill you all!" In a few minutes he calmed down, and when the police came to take him away he went peaceably.

Additional information was obtained by the prison social worker. His family is composed of father (a mason, aged 47), mother (housewife, aged 41), and a younger brother (aged 14). Only the father works. Their apartment is very small; no one has a room of his or her own.

Mario's mother comes from a large family (five brothers and sisters) and had a twin sister who died at the age of 6 months. She left school after the fifth grade; before marriage she worked at a factory job, but her husband did not want her to continue. She is often depressed, and a year earlier she was hospitalized for a while for that reason.

Mario's father attended school only up to the third grade. His mother died when he was 5 years old, and he was brought up by his older sisters and brothers. He feels he is a hard worker and prides himself on his ability to raise a family on just his own labour.

Pregnancy with Mario and his birth were regular. His mother was very proud and called the unborn boy "my great man". Breast-feeding was extremely difficult; it turned out that the milk ducts were atrophied. Mario's sleep-waking rhythm was irregular. He was an extremely active boy and often had accidents, twice fairly serious ones.

He suffered recurrent otitis, diagnosed at age 8 years. Apparently, at that time the doctor reproached Mario's mother for not having noticed it earlier, and she became very anxious over Mario's health.

His parents describe him as a very lively boy until puberty, when he grew more reserved and distant. He was also sensitive to the family's problems and tried to do something to help. At first he was extremely jealous of his brother, but now they seem to team up.

He dropped out of school, even though he had done quite well, because he had problems with a teacher. He was ashamed of his father's occupation and tried, unsuccessfully, to find a different kind of work. He spent a lot of time at home reading, mainly encyclopaedias.

The therapeutic experience with Mario took place in a juvenile detention centre. Therapeutic intervention was requested within three weeks of incarceration because of Mario's isolation, refusal of food, suicide threats, sudden aggressive acts, inability to fall asleep and early waking, and physical disturbances such as itching and eczema. The boy always asked for drugs.

At the first meeting, Mario walks in slowly, crouching slightly. He is a sturdy young man with a suspicious gaze. His words are precise and appropriate. He says he feels down because of what he has done, as he has given his parents another, and ultimate, disappointment: "They will never forgive me."

He has always hated blood. He dislikes prison above all for the lack of privacy. He says he is ashamed when he washes or goes to the bathroom. "I am very fastidious. I have refused some jobs because I don't like to get dirty. I always have to feel clean." He does not complain about his confinement, because he thinks it is right.

He seems relieved when we agree on meeting once a week. From the start, he makes me feel very important for him: "I'm in your hands. Everything depends on you." He asks about my work, saying that he knows something about psychology from the encyclopaedia. He is proud of his cultural interests and learning and says, grandiosely: "I could make a lot of money if I went on a quiz show."

The crime is invariably described as the inevitable outcome of Antonio's behaviour: "I couldn't be a coward, I had to discharge a weight. And, then, he hit me on the ear, and I've always had problems with my ears." Gradually, however, the focus of the therapy shifts to his psychic pathology. In the boy's telling of it, the crime becomes enormously grave. He asks about a woman who is in prison and the death sentence on her. He is tormented by the idea that if he lived in the United States he might risk the death sentence. He says: "I feel I am in a dark tunnel. I think it is Death Row." He complains of not being able to sleep and of lying awake at night. His feelings of sadness and depression are mainly related to what his parents think of him rather than to the crime itself.

He says that he fears retaliation by Antonio (he is afraid of leaving prison too soon), adding, "When I am in my room, in the dark, I am afraid someone is there. I keep checking every corner. And my mother says I have no sense of danger!" The fears he experiences in fantasy are a way of evoking his inner objects, alive and present, which he gradually brings to the therapeutic situation. He says: "Lately I was often at home. My mother nagged me because I didn't have a job and didn't go to school. I felt terribly ashamed. My parents have always been proud that I did well in school; my problems began when I dropped out."

"My mother was a beautiful woman. Now she is skinny, almost flat-chested. It all started with my breast-feeding. I cried, and Mamma felt bad. She couldn't feed me because the milk didn't come out of her nipple. My Grandma had the same difficulty, so that my aunt, my mother's twin sister, died when she was 6 months old from drinking infected milk. When I was a baby I was terrible. I would eat only certain types of food, I didn't sleep at night. My brother is the quiet type, although he too was bottle-fed. Papa is always at work; he comes home dirty and dead tired. When I see him in that state I get really angry, and sometimes I tell him so. But Papa is proud and doesn't want anyone's help. When he gets home he just goes to bed and sleeps. Temperamentally he is too easy-going. He told me that when he was in the army his mates wet his bed, but he didn't do anything about it, even though when he was young he was good with his fists. Often, when he was asleep, I took his car keys and went out driving around. Then I put them back in their place and he never noticed; but once I had an accident. He did not get very angry, but he didn't speak to me for nearly a month."

Once I was unable to go to the detention centre for our session, and Mario wasn't told until the last minute. The next time we met, the contents of his account were quite different. He says he doesn't want his relatives to attend the trial. "If Antonio comes, he will have to be careful what he says. My uncle knows karate and has been in jail. He's not afraid of anything or anybody." I relate his tension to the fact that the date for the trial has been set, but also to my absence at a moment when he probably felt the need to tell me about the trial. He responds that in his last talk with his parents, once the trial date was set, they talked mainly about the difficulties of an uncle of his who is a drug addict.

I tell him that it must have been hard for him to feel that he represented such a problem for his parents as to force them to talk about that instead of about himself and his worries. "I often went to Mamma and wanted to talk about myself. But I ended up asking for a little money. At night Papa was always too tired."

When he is denied parole, he says: "Well, now my room is really clean. But I can't stand my roommate Bruno. He always wants to watch porno films on TV so he can masturbate. He is not ashamed. I turn away, but one of these days I'll give him a good thrashing. I loathe him. Masturbation is good until you're 16. I haven't masturbated for a long time. At home I used to do it in the bathroom, so no one could see me. Well, I'm really telling you everything, aren't I!"

As the trial draws near, he tells me his first dream: "This dream woke me up. *I was riding a motorcycle with Bruno and maybe Sergio* [two fellow inmates]. *One of them was surely Bruno. We wore helmets. We went into a supermarket with guns. It was a robbery. Policemen came and started shooting. One policeman died, then the three of us died one after the other. I was the second to die, Bruno was the last, I am sure.* We have become friends in jail. Everybody here seems to think Bruno is stupid, and so did I at the beginning. But now I protect him. Last night I talked a lot with him. I don't know if I am an introvert or an extrovert. I don't quite get the meaning of these words. I even looked them up in the dictionary. What do you think I am? In a way I am like my father. My problem is that I do not think before acting. I realize it only after I have done something. But when you have done something, it is not like writing with a pencil. You can't erase it."

Six months after the beginning of treatment, at the last session before the trial, Mario comes in a bit late and apologizes, saying that he needed time to get ready. His voice is calm and relaxed. "I washed and shaved. Tomorrow is an important day: I decided how to dress." I think that his making me wait is an attempt to control actions, and I tell him that although he is very scared of the outcome of the trial, he has managed to find relief by getting ready and imagining what will happen.

"I used not to think about it, but now I use external signs to get clues on how the trial will go. In my room I have a puppet: it's an acrobat turning around on a string. I often ask it how things will go by giving it a turn. If it stops while showing me its back, my day will be bad; otherwise, I feel relieved. I have always been superstitious. Mamma has a book where you can find the explanation of dreams, what lottery numbers they correspond to."

I think Mario's attention to the external environment and to my reactions in the transference situation is the expression of his effort to test the existence and strength of coherent cores of the self and their relationship with self-objects. I tell him that he has now found some ways to calm down, that he can now face uncertain and difficult moments. I then ask him how he feels with me today. "This morning I woke up earlier than usual. I thought about everything. I think I am clever in some things, but sometimes I simply don't think. And then it's as if I were stupid. Before acting I should think—but I can't because I'm nervous, like everybody else at home. I didn't like Antonio, he was part of it, but I should have stopped. There were no serious motives. This morning I awoke suddenly. I was dreaming I was *in a room with the judge, we were sitting facing each other. He was neatly dressed, but I don't recall his face. He leafed through a large book slowly and carefully. Then he said my name and sentenced me to three years in jail.* That wouldn't be so wrong. Bruno killed someone and got six years. The book was very similar to my mother's book."

With reference to the dream, I tell Mario that he has been able to wait for the trial, that he is preparing himself in fantasy, so that he will be able to accept punishment, at least partially. I also talk about his ability to face adults and to judge himself. This dream is an important moment in the therapy, as thanks to the therapeutic relationship to a self-object Mario moves to a less persecutory position.

Reconstructing the story of Mario from the start, we can see that the mother–child relationship began abnormally owing to the coexistence of two conflicting conditions. On the one hand there was a narcissistic over-investment in the child ("my great man"), and on the other a malformation of the mammary ducts, accompanied by doubly negative phantasms: the hereditary defect and the death that it may bring (the mother's twin sister).

Thus death made its entry, at the fantasy level, in the mother–son relationship. It would mark Mario's psychic development profoundly, and the boy would find it impossible to distinguish between constructive aggressiveness and destructive violence. He was always trying to cope with a destructiveness that lacked all possibility of modulation, leading from rage to death as the almost automatic consequence. The archaic nature of this aggressiveness is clearly evident in Mario's fury immediately after the attack when he swears on his mother's "dead body" to kill them all. And it returns later as well, as the sense of guilt that haunts him when he thinks that he is "on Death Row". This expression inevitably calls to mind an embrace, a mortal holding, fuelled by a circular, symbiotic relationship. [In Italian, Death Row is *"braccio della morte"*, literally the "arm of death".] And in recounting his breast-feeding, Mario says, "I cried and Mamma felt bad".

The mother's failure, years later, to notice her son's otitis shows that the narcissistic circuit was still preventing her from recognizing him as an object detached from herself. This is the mother–son relationship typical of the borderline, as in the adolescents described by Masterson (1971) and Masterson and Rinsley (1975) and applied to juvenile delinquents by Marohn, Dalle Molle, McCarter, and Linn (1980).

The oedipal conflict, both when it first arises and upon its post-puberty re-enactment, is the acid test that can throw the narcissistic structure of the self into crisis. Crises may be manifested in the most variegated ways and behaviours; what they have in common, at the profound level, is fragmentation of the self (and, hence, of objects), regression, and splitting of parts of the self and of the ego, with an obvious maladjustment to external reality.

In the case of Mario, such a collapse of self during the early childhood oedipal phase can only be presumed indirectly, insofar as the brief term of therapy and the subject's limited capacity for introspection made more thorough exploration of that crucial period impossible. The strongest evidence is his early nervousness, his poorly idealized "dirty and dead tired" father-figure, and his accident proneness, presumably the product of aggressiveness directed against himself resulting from a sense of guilt.

The adolescent revival of the oedipal conflict appears to have generated unmistakable signs of a disorganization of the self: dropping out of school, maladjustment *vis-à-vis* work, isolation and introversion, attacks against his father (secret joy-riding), megalomaniacal personality traits, and the emotional reactions following his crime and his extremely primitive, almost delirious sense of guilt.

Even the determinants of the assault would appear to be deeply imbued with oedipal-linked feelings. We refer in particular to the incident outside the stadium, i.e. the sharing of an object (the banknote) that both Mario and Antonio wanted.

Antonio had stayed in school and succeeded in getting things that Mario had not (friends, a motorbike, girls, etc.). In a word, he was a good, well-behaved teenager, and socially integrated; an aggressive clash with him might well signify competing, going up against a solid, self-assured person unconsciously representing an oedipal object, a substitute for the father.

Equally oedipal is Mario's account of the time spent with his mother before the assault, although here we also see the whole passive side of the conflict, what Laufer (Laufer & Laufer, 1984) calls the "surrender of the sexual body to the mother".

Fragility of the self and the merging with the mother typical of the narcissistic personality structure predispose the subject to an inevitably passive, losing solution to the oedipal conflict. Mario's passive, fragile side emerges in the detail of the punch to his ear. True, through his history of otitis Mario is still branded by his relation of merging with his mother. But it is also true that from time immemorial the word "orecchione" (mumps, big ear) and the gesture of touching someone's ear have meant a homosexual allusion. The subject's mother-identification inevitably falls on the narcissistic wound of the perceived blockage of instinctual development, immediately prompting the fantasy of proving himself a man (i.e. slayer of the father).

In Laufer's view, the blocked development of the adolescent may take essentially two forms: deadlock, a no-exit conflict over the sexual image of the self; or foreclosure, a premature blockage that precludes achievement of the normal steps in development.

Mario's condition certainly more closely resembles deadlock; he sought to force the block by translating his fantasy into a concrete action. Consequently, the criminal episode itself can be held to be the equivalent of a psychotic crisis, demonstrating the presence of a "psychotic functioning" as described by Laufer. For when such functioning takes hold, then as in a delirium real objects take on the role of externalized persecutors, against which rage and destructiveness are directed.

Thus the homicidal assault is an attempt—admittedly, a desperate one—to safeguard a self in the process of fragmentation, an attempt by the separated self to escape disaster.

Mario's implacable rage at Antonio expresses a primal need for self-assertion, sensed as necessary to growth; not, therefore, a simple reaction to feelings of impotence, but the continuing, paradoxical hope for an empathetic response from the internal parental object, at that moment externalized.

The iron law governing the psychic economy of the narcissist, however, immediately inverts the destruction of the object into self-destruction. Whatever the actual material outcome of the fight, the subject cannot but suffer enormous psychic damage in terms of destruction of his own existence. The inability to modulate destructive aggression precludes its circumscription to castration (of self or the other); instead, castration is confused with extermination.

The guilt and anxiety found in these subjects during pre-trial detention likewise bear the mark of this primitiveness, as is eloquently attested by Mario's robbery dream, in which extermination is the only possible outcome.

Quite a different inner psychic situation is manifest in the later dream of the judge. Here we observe the effects produced by the beneficial containment worked by detention and of an empathetic relationship with an object (the therapist) totally different from those Mario had around him until that moment. The manifest content of the dream turns on the modulation of guilt, but the earlier material supplied by Mario offers a glimpse, at deeper levels, of a latent message concerning the state of the self, the relations between inner needs, the level of thought, and the capacity for symbolization.

As an instrument for establishing the correspondence between inner states and their external consequences, the penal code that the judge leafs through in the dream has a fundamental meaning in relation to the divining methods of Mario's mother. It represents Mario's hopes of finding in the therapist a new sense of his life, a new interpretation of his actions, his feelings, his situation—one different from his mother's book of dreams, with its automatic connection of dreams to numbers, or, in other words, the denial of all possibility of understanding, interpretation, comprehension in favour of magical, automatic, inexplicable answers.

The relation between the judicial system and superstitious beliefs is also clear in Mario's association of his habit of making his toy acrobat, with its tumbling, the arbiter of his fate. Now, however, he begins to discriminate, to discern what might really befall him ("They'll give me three years"). What is clear, in short, is his hesitant attempt at separation from an original maternal object that cannot be explored, known, modulated, where there is no possibility of negotiation but only an absolute answer: life or death. The acrobat's answer is that of chance, i.e. that of an omnicomprehensive and omnipotent mother figure.

At least in the unconscious, Mario is beginning to glimpse the possibility of discrimination, of an object relationship that is regulated, governed by rules. Also, we observe the transition to the reality principle by someone coming from the world of fantasy, magic, and chance, where anything at all can happen—life can turn instantly into death, there's nothing strange about that, it is the most natural thing in the world.

Reconstructing this boy's story and psychic structure in these terms, we can see just how close to psychosis it is, and how easily a borderline structure can suddenly erupt in an isolated psychotic act of criminal violence. But we also see that building a relationship, even over such a short period of time, may permit the beginnings of growth.

Paolo

> One winter afternoon, "Paolo" (age 17) was at home in a small mountain village with his mother, his grandmother, and an aunt. The grandmother was sitting by the fireplace. Paolo thought she was leaning too close to the fire, that she might fall and burn herself, so he helped her change position. His aunt scolded him, and he got angry and sent her out of the house. His mother, in turn, reproached him, asking if he was crazy.
>
> A little later, Paolo decided to clean his father's rifle, which he had done many times before but always in his father's presence. He went to the kitchen and picked up the cartridge belt. He loaded the rifle, thinking he had put it on "safety". His grandmother told him to point the barrel up, just in case it might fire. Paolo then pulled what he thought was the safety catch, but it was the trigger. The shot hit her right in the face.
>
> When he saw her covered with blood, he felt a rage and began firing wildly around, hitting his mother in the shoulder. His vision went blank then, and he no longer knew what was happening. He attacked his mother with a hunting knife. He went back to his room and took two more cartridge belts and hung them around his waist. He reloaded the rifle and, with his

mother screaming, left the house and shot a passer-by (with no idea why), slightly wounding her. He kept firing into the ground, until two cousins got to him and took the rifle. When he saw his mother bleeding, he asked her who had wounded her. When his mother replied, "You have killed me and Grandma", Paolo says he felt his mind open up again. He returned to his senses and said, "What are you telling me, Mamma? Are you crazy?" He went back home and found his grandmother dead. He called her repeatedly, then tried to reattach a flap of skin hanging from a face wound.

During pre-trial detention, Paolo had moments of all-destructive rage, fits of aggression against himself and his fellow inmates, and he refused to take part in recreational or social activities.

At the beginning of his course of weekly psychotherapy, Paolo appears self-assured. He asks me for an explanation of my professional activities and makes no effort to hide his scepticism about the usefulness of encounters with me: "What can you do with words? What have we got to say to one another? How long do we have to keep meeting?"

He claims that he does not mind detention all that much and says that he won the other inmates' respect right away with his fists. His story of himself is dominated by a magical-omnipotent type of thought and self-grandeur. "It all began with convulsive fits that none of the doctors knew how to cure. In my home village all my friends respect me and I have a girlfriend waiting for me."

The version of the murder that he relates to me is extremely implausible, bordering on mythomania. Paolo stresses his ability to control his impulses: "It was an accident. I'm sure I had the rifle on safety. It fired for no reason, all of a sudden." Gradually, his psychic pathology is taken as the reason for the therapy. Paolo expressly states his need to be contained and reassured in facing a situation that is too big for him. He complains of his difficulty in controlling impulsive reactions to the slightest comment from fellow inmates or staff. I sense that the "provocations" to which Paolo cannot avoid responding are those that stimulate his internal objects, which are alive and present; he evokes them from the very outset of treatment. He says: "I'll hit someone for the slightest insult mentioning my mother or my dead brothers. A terrible rage comes over me. Right away I feel like I'm going to faint, my vision gets cloudy, sometimes I fall to the ground. I mustn't get angry."

Of his father he says: "He never told me that he had once been a professional boxer. He would tell me to hit him in the stomach. I hurt my hands, and my father—with his hands held high—would say 'That's it? That's the best you can do?' I would go ahead, hitting him as hard as I could, but after a while he would shove me aside with a 'Sit down and stay put, or I'll smash you up against the wall'.

"Now when he comes to see me he spends just about the whole time crying. I try to comfort him, I say I'm behaving myself, but he doesn't believe me. He's so sad. He doesn't go out in the evenings any more, he doesn't go to the bar. . . . He used to stay there until late at night. I had to go and call him, plead with him to come back home, dragging him away when he was in a mood to fight with his mates.

"My parents got married when I was six. My father doesn't want my mother to leave the house by herself, so he takes care of everything: shopping, errands."

Of his mother, Paolo says she "suffers from the same attacks I do. One night I heard a blood-curdling scream. I was terribly afraid. My father came to my room and asked me to help him. My mother was on the floor, immobile. . . . My mother is the only person who ever beat me, from time to time. But I was raised by my grandparents, who treated me like a prince."

These first few references to his internal objects show the importance of Paolo's identification with his mother, who suffered from epilepsy, like him. He recalls with terror her convulsive fits; they fill him with the deepest anguish. The oedipal relationship clearly takes a negative form. The rivalry with his father is kept under control by continual declarations of admiration and the wish to be physically strong like him, but merging with the primary object is still the prevailing psychic attitude. We shall come back to this point later.

Paolo's self-image swings back and forth between a state in which he senses the internal presence of dead objects (the stillborn siblings Paolo has introjected) and a state marked by omnipotence and grandioseness, apparently moulded by his grandparents' conduct with him.

As our sessions progress, this perception of the parental images is replaced by another, one that indicates the attainment of a certain emotional distancing, possible thanks to the exclusive relationship with the therapist. Now Paolo says, "My father, if someone suggests that he do something, does the exact opposite. But if no one tells him anything, he's a good man. The other day I was really sad about Massimo [a fellow inmate] being convicted. My parents came to visit. Straight away, my mother told me I shouldn't mix with my uncle, who had no respect for her. My father kept quiet in order not to have the usual fight with Mamma on this. I was paralysed, but then I told myself, 'What have I got to do with this?' I also wanted to tell my parents that there was going to be a party here, but then I thought better of it. I was afraid they wouldn't believe me if I told them I was content here, and anyway the party was my concern only."

The role of this grandmother also begins to come clearer. For Paolo, the image of his grandmother is a protection, a source of reassurance *vis-à-vis* his parents and the outside world. Weak, ill, and dependent as she is, his grandmother is still an important object of identification. Paolo must have experienced some degree of psychic merging with her, which gave him the feeling of basic resemblance, and this, up to a point, was what sustained Paolo's fragile self. Moreover, this explains Paolo's tendency to identify with "fragile objects" as the only solution possible, so far, to the oedipal conflict.

He says: "Before, the only person I confided in was my grandmother. I spent a lot of time with her, we slept in the same room together, I tucked her in, and during the night I used to get up to get her a glass of water. When I would confide in her, she'd say, 'Don't say anything to your father, or he'll get mad'."

Now, however, Paolo recognizes himself as very lonely, fearful of leaving his home, and too shy to approach girls.

The imaginary figures of his stillborn sister and brother (they died when Paolo was 3 and then 4 years old) have a particular significance. "I've often thought that I could easily be with them. . . . Before, if someone mentioned them, I'd get so angry I couldn't see. . . . Sure, but how could the others know?" He has always forcefully defended small children, and even now, when he successfully takes their side, he says that he has "found the light again".

Paolo displays a powerful tendency to act, to go into action, when feelings of tension or anguish emerge. Yet his capacity to recognize his guilt, to sustain and develop a relationship hinging on feelings of sadness and desire for "redemption", suggests that therapy is possible.

After six months of treatment the risk of psychotic development, which had been a real threat at first, appeared to have been averted. The possibility of depression that had been observed testified to the presence of sufficiently cohesive nuclei of the self. Paolo's self-mutilating behaviour during the initial period of detention, consisting mainly of wounds to his hands, indicated on the one hand the prevalence of a poor self-image and weak present object investment. On the other hand, however, it may also have represented an attempt to limit anguish and guilt to parts of the bodily self, and thus to prevent them from also overflowing in suicidal directions or massive psychosomatic discharges like this initial convulsive attack. In any event, this behaviour indicated the great need, at that time, for positive contributions from outside, of good self and object images.

During this period, Paolo related the following dream: "I had another dream of the accident. This time I was just very angry. Aside from my aunt, Mamma and Grandma, an uncle of mine was also there. They all agreed to leave. My uncle didn't get angry; instead he said he understood my state of mind. 'Don't get mad, we're going', he said. I was happy."

This dream indicates a first movement away from the merging in which Paolo was caught up, which had become persecutory, as during the murder itself, when all these female figures seemed to have coalesced against him. It was this state of persecution that Paolo was trying to escape, at the moment of breakdown, through his murderous acting out. Escape had now become possible thanks to the therapeutic relationship. I limited my interpretation to the emergence of a less primitive male identification and the simultaneous rise of hopes of restoring his confidence in the outside environment.

After twelve months of treatment, Paolo's attitudes and his life in the detention centre had changed greatly. He was working regularly at the craft workshop, cultivating a small vegetable garden with pleasure, and taking part in social life. He enjoyed a certain reputation, being considered an old-timer at the jail, or what draftees in the army would call a "grandfather". This revaluation of the "grandfather" figure, which in a sense Paolo could now impersonate in real life, seemed important. Now he could transform the weak, dependent part of the self that had developed through his identification with his grandparents into something powerful and authoritative. These internal objects thus acquired a new, positive meaning, reducing Paolo's narcissistic vulnerability and reinforcing his self-image.

Now his changes in mood were less sudden, less frequent. Fights and moments of rage were isolated episodes and less intense. Paolo was taking good care of his room, which signified a greater investment in self. He was neat, clean, and tidily dressed, and he was taking classes towards his junior-high-school diploma.

Thanks to the increased self-esteem that came from feeling appreciated and listened to, and the availability of the therapist as an object of idealization and identification, the therapeutic relationship had permitted a reduction of his aggressive drives.

Paolo had also begun to bring the gravity of the events into the framework of his own responsibility. While right from the start he had said that he was sorry and felt sad about the "accident", the quality of his sadness and a capacity to cope with depression with less massive use of archaic defence mechanisms (splitting, idealization, omnipotence, denial) now indicated that a mourning process had surely been initiated.

As for job plans, after a phase marked by mainly imitative identification with me and other prison personnel, when he said that he would like to be an activity group leader or a guard, Paolo went back to his original desire of being a car mechanic. The significance of this in terms of "reparation" is evident, but this choice also indicated that through therapy a healthy need for authentic self-assertion had re-emerged.

Towards the end, he would often remain silent during our sessions, saying that he had no desire to say anything. "I was often alone before, too. Secretly I used to go up a hill near our village. Here, now, I openly say that I want to be alone. I no longer want to tell everybody, superficially, what happened to me. I feel that I can stay still and silent."

As his trial drew near, Paolo displayed a new need to "know" how things had really gone, demonstrating his continuing need to try himself, in fantasy, but at the same time to check his progress and be able to feel ready to face not only the judicial process but also his own inner process of growth.

He had an extremely significant dream. "*I was together with a lot of my family, up before the judge. He read out a guilty verdict. Strangely, I didn't feel discouraged or afraid. Calmly I told the judge that he hadn't understood my feelings, what I really felt. I was taken to a room filled with light, but there weren't any bars on the windows or iron doors. In the room there was a woman and two children. I felt a sense of satisfaction, and even though I knew of the sentence, I didn't feel convicted.*"

Obviously, such successful expression of one's own point of view embodies the hope of being able to make oneself understood, not just that of being understood, and thus demonstrates a more advanced object relationship.

After fifteen months of therapy, the trial was held. Paolo was convicted and sentenced to six-and-a-half years. He took the sentence with composure, and later said: "Everyone told me I behaved like a man."

In therapy, Paolo appears to bring the figure of the therapist and that of the judge together in fantasy, a clear attempt to attenuate the splitting between good and bad objects. This enables him to contain his destructive attitudes while also indicating the activation of specific needs for idealization, which his identification with me now allows.

In seeking to reconstruct the story of Paolo, another of his dreams may be a useful starting point. "I was with two friends. We come to an old, tumble-down church. A custodian shows us in. Inside it is empty—the church is abandoned. I find a drawer with a pen and a ring in it. I pick up the pen and at that moment everything begins to shake. I leave everything in the drawer. We run away. I find myself at a friend's house. We are met by his parents. They are nice. They offer me a room that I can have all to myself. In it there are two beds. I feel happy."

At the time of his homicidal incident, Paolo had reached a saturation level of anguish, threatening the collapse of his psychic structure. His efforts at emancipation had failed; his parents were dangerous objects, being incapable of bearing and raising children; his castration anxiety took on a tinge of persecution. Paolo, the sole surviving child, was born "very small, very small"; he knows he is diseased, he has epileptic attacks. In short, he finds himself in Laufer's "deadlock" (Laufer & Laufer, 1984), in which all possibilities of growth appear to be cut off.

The figure of his grandmother, which until that moment had served as a protective shield against the stimuli deriving from his dangerous parental images, was suddenly undone in that role. Thus the attempt to take up the rifle–pen–penis (i.e. to gain an unquestioned masculine identity, integrating his sexual body into his self-image) provokes a breakdown, as the necessity of growth is so urgent that procrastination is no longer possible.

Before his murderous fit, in fact, Paolo's amorous investments were non-existent. "I was obsessed by the idea that I would turn all red and have an attack if I approached a girl." He was also terrified by the reactions that masturbation could produce, associating orgasm with a convulsive attack. These fears are evident in a recurrent dream of Paolo's during the early part of his detention. *"A girl wants me to kiss her, she comes near me. Suddenly the earth starts to shake and I wake up in terror."* Only towards the end did Paolo talk, with reserve, of his sexual desires and his masturbatory activity.

At the moment of the murder, then, Paolo acted out a fantasy of magic psychic growth in which killing his grandmother meant maniacally freeing himself from his infantile self-image and at the same time attacking the women–mothers who wanted to keep him tied down; this acting out was modelled on the style of the omnipotent father.

The murder episode, in short, displays a "psychotic functioning". The destructiveness of the homicidal action comes subsequent to the indifferent, objectless discharge of aggression represented by his epileptic fits, which began two years earlier, but it also constitutes the transcendence of such discharge in that it involves an external object. The homicidal action, in this interpretation, is the abandonment of a situation of "epileptic rupture of the self", to quote Masud Khan (1983), in favour of a desperate attempt to safeguard a self that was undergoing fragmentation.

Over the course of therapy, both Paolo's behaviour in the sessions (making me wait for him) and his violent fights with other inmates more and more clearly suggest the possibility of controlling his actions. Moreover, his keen attention to my reactions and those of the external environment to his actions represents an effort to test the existence and the solidity of a separate self that had escaped the catastrophe and of its relationships with self-objects, as defined by Kohut (1971).

The therapeutic relationship enabled Paolo to revisit his impulsive act both as a response to his recognition of his own extreme vulnerability and as a desperate way of seeking to grow and cope with the danger of total annihilation of self.

In these circumstances, therapeutic technique relied very little on interpretation (which remained internal to the therapist's own psyche) and was deliberately based on self-object transference to encourage the development of narcissistic charges.

Paolo's personal history does not appear to reveal, in his childhood, affective deprivation severe enough to explain his frequent, intense aggressive reactions or his narcissistic vulnerability. Nevertheless, the murder itself and the other acts of violence can be read in the light of the episode in which Paolo punched his father in the stomach. Far from the acting out of the oedipal conflict, what that situation expressed was the primal need for self-affirmation, sensed as necessary to growth. That is, the attack on the father in this case was not a reaction to a sense of impotence but continuing hopes in an empathetic response from an object whose function is to safeguard the integrity of the self. From this viewpoint, we can more easily explain Paolo's surprise and satisfaction when he discovered that he was understood and accepted by the therapist.

Discussion

The detailed accounts of these two cases show clearly, in our view, that the psychopathology of these patients can be diagnosed as an "antisocial personality disorder". Yet they also display unmistakable traits of narcissistic pathology; these are more obvious in the case of Paolo, whose psychic organization has a number of evident borderline features.

Both patients displayed a clearly passive attitude towards the oedipal conflict being re-enacted in the adolescent phase. Structural inconsistency of the self, archaic defence mechanisms, and the impossibility of taking advantage of good object relationships induced both boys to seek to resolve unconscious conflicts by action rather than psychic elaboration. In both cases, the high degree of narcissistic rage, weak instinctual fusion, and the failure of ego integration explain the destructiveness of the aggressive drive. Conditions like these have led theorists of the death instinct to speak of a "death constellation" (Williams, 1983). Also, the unstable balance of object and narcissistic cathexes accounts for the sudden reversal of aggressive discharge from its object back to the subject (a suicidal attitude for Mario; a self-aggressive one for Paolo).

Reviewing the psychoanalytic contributions to criminal psychology, beginning with Freud (1916d, 1925f), we find that they all focus on the symbolic meaning of the criminal act, on the unconscious conflicts underlying it, and on the significance that acting out illegal behaviour can assume with respect to a preexisting relation.

Recent progress in the understanding of narcissistic pathology, however, has resulted in a fundamental shift in emphasis from the psychodynamics of the criminal act to the psycho-economic perspective. This helps us to detect and understand episodes of fragmentation of the self, as well as the defences that the subject deploys to preserve or restore the cohesion and equilibrium of the self.

It is well known that adolescents with primitive narcissistic personalities try to reconstitute a crumbling self by actively converting an injury into an assault, utilizing a familiar behaviour pattern of destructiveness (Marohn, 1994; Marohn et al., 1980). Yet there are cases in which violent destructive behaviour is not associated with any well-defined thoughts, wishes, or fantasies. Such episodes appear not to be associated with any content, or psychodynamic meaning. While rage-like behaviour may follow an experience that does have psychodynamic significance and ends in fragmentation, the behaviour itself merely represents the disintegrated condition; in some instances, it may represent an effort to reorganize the self by restoring its primacy.

This proposition suggested to one of the authors that sometimes, in acts of violent assault/destructive discharge against his victim, the adolescent enacts a particular unconscious fantasy. These adolescents realize that their psychic growth is stymied, and they fantasize overcoming this deadlock at a stroke, leaping over the entire gap separating them from the prized objective of a more adult status. This objective may be represented, for instance, by a more advanced phase of sexual development, by more direct investment in an extra-family object, or by more mature ego and superego functions. The magic act of violence is, in any event, manifested in a way that corresponds to the features of omnipotent thought and the grandiose self. In many cases, violent behaviour of spectacular self-assertion and a caricature of hypervirility or hyperfemininity disclose symbolic details that betray the unconscious purpose underlying the act.

Notwithstanding the utter unacceptability of the attempt, it can be argued that in the acts provoked by such fantasies these adolescents reveal at least one legitimate wish: psychological growth. And this is an element that no one interested in rehabilitating juvenile delinquents can afford to underestimate. This presumed fantasy has accordingly been labelled the "psychic growth fantasy" (Novelletto, 1986, 1988).

We believe that once verified in the adolescent criminal's transference onto his therapist and received by the latter in his countertransference, this fantasy can be helpful in establishing an empathic relationship. Narcissistic rage cannot be treated directly. The therapist must address the empathic rupture that has taken place between the patient and his self-object, causing the destructive discharge. To do so, the therapist himself must re-establish the empathic relation with the adolescent and offer himself as self-object, a substitute for the originals.

In both cases presented here, the period of post-arrest and pretrial detention were crucial for evaluating the possibility of self-object transference onto the therapist. This possibility, which can emerge only from a regular, continuous relation, is crucial both for diagnosis (assessment of self-cohesion, reality testing, and preconscious functioning) and prognosis (evaluation of the possible change through the ongoing psychological relation). Moreover, thanks to the cooperation of prison staff and the sound daily organization of both of these boys' lives, detention allowed the creation of a consistent therapeutic setting whose progressive internalization acted as a shield against external as well as inner stimuli.

From the therapeutic standpoint, we think that for quite a long period of treatment the therapist must absolutely take account of these patients' demands for attention and recognition as signs of the re-enactment of the grandiose self, in Kohut's (1971) sense. The principal therapeutic effect deriving from the transference condition brought about by the enactment of the grandiose self is the possibility for the patient to re-enact and maintain a process that can be worked through in which the analyst is used as a therapeutic "buffer". This allows the progressive harnessing on non-ego-syntonic fantasies and narcissistic impulses. In other words, the key function of specular transference is to reproduce a condition that actively facilitates the spontaneous development of the patient's narcissistic cathexes towards an objectal type of choice.

A particular feature of our therapeutic approach in these cases was active association—for example, between the patients' accounts of their serious antisocial acts and the related fantasy life. Associations were structured according to a set of theoretical assumptions that gradually made it possible to define, discuss, and transform into narrative something that threatened instead to crystallize within the mind as a mere discharge of acts. This practice performed a function of external symbolization, which substituted for and was conceived as a support to the patients' own processes of symbolization. Both patients responded with an idealizing transference onto the therapist, which we considered as the re-emergence of parental omnipotence, a requisite for the child to feel safe in the presence of his parents. One sign of this phase was a series of sessions in which the patients were silent, declaring that they did not want to say anything. These were quiet moments, in which the therapists felt that the boys did not want to be pressed. Masud Khan (1983) has described a peculiar psychological condition as "lying fallow" like a field to be sown the next year. This is an intimate, non-conflictual, personalized area of self-experience, a healthy ego function that the subject can use. This relates to Winnicott's concept (1967) of a child being alone in the presence of his mother, alone with himself in a quiet state of well-being. We think that in cases like these, if the treatment goes well, these are moments in which the patients let us know that their childhood did not offer them any such experience.

CHAPTER SIX

An invitation to a journey: the function of the double in the psychoanalytic psychodrama of a psychotic adolescent

Alain Gibeault

The child was playing
with a small wooden cart
He realized he was playing
And said, I am two!

There is one to play
And another to know;
One sees me play
And the other sees me see.

I am behind me
But if I turn my head
I'm no longer where I wanted to be
Turning around does that . . .

F. Pessoa, "The Child Was Playing" (1977)

The double is a constitutive element of the functioning of the psyche, haunted by the repetition of *oneness* in hallucinatory wish-fulfilment while at the same time obliged to negotiate this quest for the absolute by accepting the repetition of *sameness*. It is this dialectic between the search for perceptual identity and the search for thought identity that Freud described when he wrote about dreams. It is at the centre of the human adventure that emerges from the discovery of the unconscious and of psychic conflict. From this perspective, the problematic of the double—so often described in myths and in literature—is a good illustration of the contradiction inherent in psychic life between the need to overcome death by striving for eternity and immortality and the need to accept time and finitude in order to deal with anxiety about death. Freud indicated this when he described the double as being at one and the same time "an insurance against the destruction of the ego" and a "harbinger of death" (1919h, p. 235).

The experience of psychoanalysis, based as it is on free association and the suspension of visual and motor activity during the sessions, reveals the simultaneous functioning of two modes of thought: that of dreaming—the search for perceptual identity—and that of wakefulness, which corresponds to the work of thought identity. When the fundamental rule is stipulated, it engenders an uncanny anxiety arising from the loss of limits, the vacillation of identity. Hypercathexis of the analyst as an external double makes it possible to fight against these anxieties related to formal and topographical regression (cf. Botella & Botella, 1984). Psychoanalysis on the couch is the preferred treatment for patients who are able to confront these anxieties without running the risk of pathological disorganization and regression.

It is not the same for those for whom a face-to-face psychotherapy is recommended. It is thought that in those cases visual and motor props are necessary for psychic work to be tolerable and possible. A different form of psychotherapy—individual psychodrama—introduces still another variation in setting and technique. The paradox of psychoanalytic psychodrama lies in systematically prescribing in play form that which is elsewhere considered to hinder the development of the psychoanalytic process, and in particular the lateralization of the transference and acting-out, either physically or verbally. It is true that doing this in a playful mode circumvents the kind of resistance involved in defences such as acting-out, thus turning it into a very special mode of elaboration for patients who would not be able to tolerate a transferential relationship organized around a single analyst. While, in psychodrama, the dynamic of the process (transference) and the aims remain the same as in classical analysis, nonetheless there are differences that arise from the setting.

In this chapter I refer to individual psychoanalytic psychodrama as theorized by Lebovici, Diatkine, and Kestemberg (1958), Kestemberg (1958), Kestemberg and Jeammet (1981, 1987), Gillibert (1985), and Amar, Bayle, and Salem (1988). Individual psychoanalytic psychodrama provides the economic and topographical conditions for interpretations to be heard without intrusion, and thereby to be introjected. We are talking about a psychodrama centred on an individual patient. Also present is a group of therapists, including the leader who does the interpreting and a minimum of four co-therapists, evenly divided between the sexes, who are the potential players. The weekly sessions last half an hour.

Psychodrama is recommended for adults, adolescents, or children who are either very excitable or very inhibited. These are often characteristics of psychotic functioning or of a period of intense change as in pre-adolescence or adolescence. The leader and the different members of the group present sufficient diversity to permit the enormous transferential investment to be fragmented and thus to reduce the economic weight of this excitation. Optimally, the alternation of interpretation within and outside the play leads to a concentration of the displaced or ambivalent psychic movement on the person of the leader. When this happens, the transference can be handled as in psychoanalytic treatment with a single analyst.

In working to constitute the psychic topography in patients with a poorly functioning preconscious, psychodrama relies on the representation of the double which can be both *represented* by a psychodramatist during the play as well as *signified* by the leader of the play. The distribution of functions facilitates the emergence and toleration of affects such as feelings of the uncanny and the loss of a sense of boundaries, often denied and split. If the psychodramatists and the one who plays the double can refer to the functioning of perceptual identity, the leader can introduce a reference to thought identity.

What is the double in psychodrama? In this collective "dream work" that is the characteristic of psychodrama, the double's function is to evoke the patient in the first person, to introduce a voice that expresses the drives, fantasies, and representations that the person cannot express himself. The function of the group of psychodramatists is to assume the different aspects of the instinctual life and the psychic agencies of the patient. The use of the first person takes on a special meaning because it makes recognition and subsequent narcissistic support possible. Voice-off or mirror play make it easier to utilize the concept of the time of *illusion* of a found/created object and to make possible at a later point the time of *disillusionment* and the acceptance of the object in its otherness (Winnicott, 1971).

There is, of course, always the risk of a coincidental identity between what the patient is feeling and what the therapist as the double is playing. This introduces a possibly traumatic element. Freud refers to this when he wrote: "An uncanny effect is often and easily produced when the distinction between imagination and reality is effaced, as when something that we have hitherto regarded as imaginary appears before us in reality, or when a symbol takes over the full functions of the thing it symbolizes" (Freud, 1919h, p. 244). This "magical" dimension of psychodrama is mediated by the role of the leader, who can, as a third party, interject space between "that's the way it is" and "that's not the way it is", the difference between oneness and sameness.

The use of psychodrama to treat "Pascal", a very inhibited preadolescent, provides clinical material that will permit me to illustrate the importance of a setting that not only offers visual and physical outlets, but also the representation of the double. It is thus that a psychoanalytic process becomes a possibility.

Example

Pascal was 10 years old when he came to us for psychodrama. He was first seen in the clinic at age 5 when his parents brought him because of two convulsive episodes at the beginning of each of two nursery-school years. He remained mute during the consultation and played with toy animals for a while, setting them up in violent combat. Then he lapsed into an attitude of frozen indifference. Twice-weekly psychotherapy was proposed, and this treatment lasted two and a half years. There did not seem to be any real change; he repeated the same scenes of violent combat and remained indifferent to the words of his therapist, most particularly when reference was made to his anger over the primal scene. The therapy was ended because Pascal did not wish to come any more and because the therapist felt immobilized and dull.

The parents requested a consultation two years later, at which time a trial psychodrama was initiated in a group co-led by René Diatkine and myself.* Pascal was very inhibited with us too; he never suggested a scene that we could play. He never assigned the parts. He would give the same answers each time: "I don't know", "I don't care". He seemed to be under the sway of a fantasy of traumatic seduction which left him no alternative other than to adopt a megalomaniac attitude of refusing to play act. The only thing possible for us to do was to play as a double, to be a voice in the first person which might permit him to have a fantasized representation that could be projected under the watchful eye of a third person, the leader, whose interpretative activity had the function both of a protective shield and of binding. I shall illustrate this with material from several sessions at intervals of several months apart after two years of psychodrama, and then describe some more recent sessions.

As always, René Diatkine, the leader, began by asking Pascal, "What shall we play?", and as always Pascal answered, "I don't know". Conforming to a pattern adopted at the beginning of the psychodrama, I intervened to play his double and said: "Last night I had a bizarre dream. *I was in a beautiful house, more beautiful than mine,* or was it mine? You know how in dreams it's not always clear. *Then I opened a door and I saw a dead person—knifed. I could have been accused of doing it.*" Pascal asked me: "And what did you do?" I answered: "I woke up. It was a

*This case is written up on the basis of notes taken by Hede Menke and Isabelle Beguier, for which I thank them.

nightmare." Stepping out of his muteness, he questioned me further about this dream: "What did he look like?" I answered: "I am not quite sure, but it was someone with grey hair." The leader sent a colleague to play the role of a third person, a friend or a mother. She said "Stop scaring him, your story is awful, I can't stand dreams like that because afterwards I am not sure whether they are true or not." I answered: "I can't stand them either; that's why I woke up." Diatkine stopped the scene and asked Pascal: "Did you like what was just played?" "Not really", answered Pascal. Diatkine said: "I noticed that. During the scene, you moved away from the two people. Do you have nightmares?" "Yes", answered Pascal, "but worse than that one." As Pascal was unable to relate his dreams, Diatkine went on: "Some things in life are frightening—death and a situation where two people hurt each other mortally." Pascal then associated: "Sometimes I dream that I am dead and that I am not in my dream."

It would seem that Pascal had anxieties about not existing, that he might lose himself just as he lost objects he cathected. His inhibition was a translation of this impossibility of cathecting an object which is so overwhelmingly exciting that neither displacement nor any other movement is possible; psychic functioning is destroyed rather than promoted. That is why it is important to be able to represent this narcissistic double for a patient who has no double in his dreams, no representation of himself in the narcissistic regression of sleep. It enables him to have a bond with an object at a comfortable distance. From this point of view, psychodrama is an attempt to dream collectively, a process whose guarantor is the leader.

Another session, a few months later, illustrates how psychodrama can create an intermediate area of experience that contributes to the foundation of all fantasizing. Diatkine greeted Pascal: "I always ask you the same question and you always give me the same answer. I propose that we play two people who surprise each other." Pascal agreed, and I approached him without any preconceived idea. I said: "Do you see the ditch over there?", pointing to the distance separating us from the other psychodramatists. "I have already jumped across it. You don't believe me, do you?" "No." So I answered him: "Do you want me to show you how I did it?" "Yes", he responded. I pretended to leap away from him and towards the other psychodramatists. I then asked him if he wanted to try too. Pascal, immobile and glued to the wall since the beginning of the psychodrama, came forward, leapt, and joined me with a self-satisfied air. I said: "You see, the impossible became possible." To our surprise, he associated to this, and said: "Then there might be a rainbow without rain, or rain without clouds. We are on another planet." From this session on, a journey "beyond the mirror" began, one that has continued ever since and has permitted Pascal to take part in imaginary scenes, testifying to his new-found capacity to tolerate a primal scene that would not necessarily lead to destruction or violent death. This is how we interpret his reference to the rainbow which, after the storm, represents the reunion of two contradictory elements—the earth and the sun. Pascal, of course, tried to separate them, but he could from then on allow himself to represent them on that "other planet" which is the scene of the psychodrama. The use of the represented double, which had been able to survive the challenge of time and violence, probably was the principal element of this treatment, which enabled him to face the "leap" of death and castration without fearing destruction.

During these trips to imaginary far-away countries, Pascal and I, his faithful companion, met a woman who offered us something to eat. After momentary distrust, Pascal wondered if "this food might be something very special". I answered: "I would like it to make me invulnerable." He associated, as in fairy tales: "I would like this food to transform me into anything I want." Diatkine interrupted the game and pointed out to Pascal that this meeting might have something to do with what a child expects from his mother. In the following session, the meeting with this unusual and wonderful woman continued: she provided "magical fruits", talismans that offered protection against all kinds of dangers, fearsome monsters, and death. And yet as soon as this woman disappeared, the enchanted world could disappear. During this scene, the person playing this woman stepped out of the scene, and Diatkine intervened to ask Pascal what he thought of it. Pascal immediately responded: "She left just at the moment that I wanted to ask her a question." We started the play again, and Pascal asked her: "If you leave, will you come back?"

Clearly the wish for immortality and invulnerability is immediately breached by the risk of absence and decathexis. Pascal gave us this impression of his whole psychoanalytic adventure. Although he came regularly to his sessions and established a continuity of cathexis leading to many important changes, he remained very susceptible to absences and vacation breaks. He might freeze up again, no longer know why he was coming, forget the game of the wonderful "lady", no longer even wish to come.

It is possible for us to imagine what was psychologically at stake in Pascal's life. He was born while his parents were in mourning; a situation of reciprocal mother–child decathexis in which the "dead mother" (Green, 1980) interacted with a "dead child", who was inhibited and immobilized by the anxiety of non-representation. The loss of the object was really the loss of the capacity to cathect an object and to "dream" with it.

Psychodrama was probably able to offer Pascal the "function of reverie" (Bion) which enabled him to make sense of his own psychic life and to play with his imagination. Recently, almost a year after the last material, Pascal suggested that he was conflicted over continuing. In my role as the double, I spoke of the conflict between the wish to stop coming and that of being sure that one was still expected. I evoked the pleasure I had found in dreaming here. Pascal associated to this by saying that he had fewer nightmares. Diatkine pointed out that "the psychodrama here is like a dream that has no end. This could upset you because there do not seem to be any limits." With remarkable pertinence, Pascal answered: "Dreaming enables one to sleep well." "And the nightmares?", asked Diatkine. "I don't have them because I wake up", said Pascal. The leader answered: "You wake up, and afterwards you remember that you had a bad dream."

It seemed that Pascal remembered my own associations of one and a half years ago on waking up from a nightmare as a triumph over anxiety and terror. If at other times he had been outside the dream presentations, our "collective dream" based on the dimension of a double that was both represented and signified had permitted him to rediscover the pleasure of dreaming, a sign of the recovery of his psychic functioning.

We understood only later to what degree any change and any break involved a risk of death for him—his own death, and the death of his mother, as could be inferred from the convulsions at the beginnings of the school year. That is why the parents consulted the clinic in the first place, probably suffering themselves from feelings of the uncanny before the "hidden forces" that seemed to inhabit their son at moments of separation which were experienced as terror. Freud reminded his readers that in the Middle Ages it was thought that epilepsy and madness were a consequence of demonic activity, and that psychoanalysis might appear "uncanny" because it was "concerned with laying bare these hidden forces" (Freud, 1919h, p. 243).

The psychodrama with Pascal revealed that the fight against these hidden forces could induce psychic inertia and monotonous repetition as safeguards against psychic, if not real, death. Psychodrama offered a fantasized exit out of this violent rigid alternation between murder and death. It offered an imaginary journey with an imagined companion who, albeit uncanny, nonetheless made it possible for Pascal to reacquire the "potential space of play" (Winnicott, 1971), the possibility to cathect positively, and a belief in the possibility of dreaming with and about an object.

Even though in our own clinical discussions we evoked the mother's depression and the succession of unsatisfactory nurses during Pascal's early childhood, this was not at the heart of our interpretative activity. We were more engaged in a construction of an experienced present time that would permit Pascal to find a truth, a contact with himself, by means of emotions and representations that he could perceive as belonging to him. He remained mistrustful both in the choice of scenes and of psychodramatists insofar as these choices might result in life or death. But if for a long time he confounded dream and reality, he had now acquired the possibility of saying to himself, "This was only play"; thanks to this compromise, he could begin to reappropriate his wishes and affects. There is still a long way to go before he can leave his external double in order to leap over the precipice by himself. One can imagine that access to the dimension of play and illusion would permit him to substitute an internal double for the external one, and then one day to discover the universe and its distant planets with greater tranquillity and pleasure.

CHAPTER SEVEN

Factors contributing to the psychotic breakdown of three adolescents

Hélène Dubinsky

This chapter looks at a constellation of emotional factors that I have observed in a number of psychotic and borderline adolescents. In the internal world of these adolescents, the mother was unable to contain her child's emotional experience, whereas the father was rejecting and at times cruel. These young people had clearly introjected a parental couple unable to help or protect their child's growth. Unsupported by good internal parents, the vulnerability of these adolescents was further compounded by feeling threatened and deprived by rivalrous internal siblings.

The experience of adolescence was found by these emotionally fragile young people to be overwhelming. They felt engulfed by confusion and anxiety as they were subjected to the surge of sexual feelings and the pressing need to define their identity as potential adults. Traumatic events in their external lives also contributed to their eventual breakdown.

I shall discuss the psychotherapy of three such adolescent patients. "Debbie" and "Tania" shared a mental image of their fathers as harshly spurning them while favouring the mother and siblings. Debbie's feelings of ill-treatment by her father left her prey to incessant thoughts of sadistic intercourse which she was increasingly unable to distinguish from reality. Tania carried her feelings of worthlessness, deprivation, and jealousy into her other relationships. Her delusional jealousy of her boyfriend brought about continual outbursts of violence. A third patient, "Thomas", whom I discuss in some detail, found growing into a man terrifying, indeed impossible. He was paralysed by his own oedipal phantasies in which he merged into a mother-figure, only to be attacked by a vengeful, rivalrous father and siblings.

Debbie

Debbie was referred to the clinic at the age of 18 years. She had been diagnosed as schizophrenic following a psychotic breakdown. She looked younger than her age and, with her round face and charming smile, had the appearance of a country girl. When I saw Debbie for an assessment, she told me, in a chatty tone, about her breakdown and her hallucinations. She spoke in a somewhat detached manner, which suggested that this was a story she was accustomed to telling, but she also conveyed amazement at the events she recounted. It was as if she was telling me about some bizarre and very unpleasant adventure that had unexpectedly befallen her.

It had started when she had to sit her mock A-levels and she heard voices coming out of the classroom light-bulbs giving her orders. She could not sleep in her bed because she believed it was full of corpses. Her behaviour became odd. She thought she was being spied on by everyone around her, that others knew what she was thinking. She was convinced that she was being followed.

Debbie's parents had worked hard to provide their three children with a good education, but they appeared to be unable to offer much in the way of emotional understanding. Debbie was the middle child of three girls. She had been lonely in her first secondary school, where she felt isolated from the other girls, who were from a more middle-class background. Her parents took her diffidence and depression for laziness and suddenly transferred her, without warning, to another school, where she felt even more isolated. She was very lonely and felt she was "crap". For a few weeks she went out with a boy who had a motorbike and who behaved roughly towards her, sometimes shouting abuse at her or hitting her.

It was when Debbie was under the pressure of school examinations that she first became very ill. Her parents apparently interpreted her mental disturbance as ill-will on her part. Having had to drop out of school and being too unwell to work, she was always at home. Her mother reproached her for putting on weight. Her father sometimes shouted at her and told her bitterly that she was good for nothing.

Debbie, who seems always to have been a fragile child, felt that she lost her parents' attention and protection early in life. She recounted how her father drank and on a few occasions became violent, mainly towards her mother. She had overheard many scenes between them. As a child, Debbie had also witnessed her mother in a frightening accident, seeing her falling under a moving bus. Following this, her mother had spent several months in hospital and seems to have been emotionally withdrawn for a long period. Shortly after her mother's accident, Debbie became the victim of bullying at school.

In the therapy material, it can be seen how Debbie's experience of her mother's accident, the bullying, and her sense of not being valued by her family, especially by her father, all contributed to her psychotic breakdown. She felt devalued and helpless but was completely out of contact with her own rage and jealousy towards others as she suffered what were perceived as constant rejections and deprivations. She projected her own aggression into men and bullies, both in her phantasy worlds and in external reality. Painful and frightening similarities between her two worlds became increasingly blatant. In her phantasy world, she was absorbed in violent, exciting phantasies in which she was the victim. In real life, she became an easy target for playground bullies and later for her abusive boyfriends.

Following our initial assessment, there was a short interval, and by the time of Debbie's first session she was back in a psychotic state. She was neither seeing nor hearing me, and her way of staring seemed mad. She looked at the corners of the room with frightened, bulging eyes and seemed to be hallucinating. The only time that she appeared to be aware of my presence was when I reconfirmed that I would continue to see her for therapy.

Soon afterwards, Debbie was put on medication by her GP. I began seeing her for therapy first once and then twice a week. She managed to come on her own to every session, despite the fact that she continued to hallucinate for a few weeks. She was increasingly able to tell me about the voices she heard: her cigarette, for example, was telling her she was a "slag". She continually feared she was being followed.

After some weeks, Debbie stopped hallucinating. She would talk in a repetitive way, going over painful little events from her everyday life: her friends had not phoned her; her parents criticized her relentlessly. Debbie also began to talk about her increasing despair at her loneliness and isolation. She felt that she was a failure. She wanted to be like everyone else and would ask why no one wanted to see her. Why didn't she have a boyfriend like everyone else? She was ashamed of still being a virgin. She was upset at having lost a Saturday job because she was too slow, too bizarre. She attempted various academic courses but would have to pull out as she was unable to concentrate or mix with others. During this initial period of Debbie's therapy, I felt that the sessions were being used by her as a place where she could dump her feelings of inadequacy so that I could hold them for her and help her process them.

In Debbie's second year of therapy, she was more absorbed in her daydreams, which were becoming increasingly violent. She appeared to be living on the edge of an abyss and was again hallucinating from time to time. The sessions felt slow, empty, heavy. There were periods when she communicated her fear of her daydreams, but the next moment she was looking at me with fixed, empty, and absent eyes, apparently not hearing me.

She would smile oddly and come back to herself, and me, and briefly recount daydreams in which she was usually the victim of violent sexual aggression. When she came out of her ruminations, she was deeply shocked by their content and would ask herself why she was ceaselessly tormented by these horrible thoughts. She was very confused about whether these things had actually happened to her or not.

When we would have to interrupt the therapy for holidays, she would fly into a rage as she discussed her parents and her past. She would pace around the therapy room, shouting and hitting on the door violently, yelling and criticizing her parents for wanting her to leave home. At a more unconscious level, she was shouting at me for leaving her between sessions, which felt to her like an abandonment. She was also shouting about all that had happened to her: her breakdown, her "crap" life, her being a victim, her conviction (recanted later when she was better) that she had been raped at different ages by different men. Most of all she shouted at the unfairness of it all. Why had all this happened to her and not her sisters, who were normal? She was consumed by envy. She felt that she had nothing while others had everything. She was tormented by her belief that her sisters got more from her parents than she did, and perhaps also that my other patients got more from me—so little was ever left for her.

In a session from this second year, Debbie began by being completely silent. Then there were the familiar long pauses in which she was absent, and I had to call her back from her own cut-off world. She finally managed to tell me about the daydream she was having. She was imagining that *she was dancing with Jack*. (I knew from other sessions that Jack was the violent boyfriend of one of Debbie's acquaintances and the father of a small baby.) In this daydream, *Jack told Debbie the baby was dead, then he kissed her and smiled at her*. After a silence, Debbie said that her father often shouted that she was "bloody useless", and once he hit her and told her she wasn't normal and would never have a boyfriend.

I felt that Debbie was showing herself to be identified both with the aggressor who kills the defenceless baby and also with the attacked and humiliated baby. In her daydream, Debbie's oedipal jealousy of the parental couple and their child was felt to have killed the baby as she acted in seductive collusion with the violent father, Jack. This kind of phantasy also showed the terrible muddle Debbie was in as she confused sexuality and destructiveness, the making and the killing of babies. Then, in a reversal typical of sado-masochism, Debbie herself became the attacked baby. Her father, like the violent Jack, turned his destructiveness against his child by hitting and humiliating her. This session allows us to see how Debbie had internalized the cruel and rejecting father figure and, further, perversely needed approval from, and closeness to, such a man.

In another session, Debbie asked me in a puzzled way: "Why do I think all the time that I have been attacked? I always dream about people who don't want to know me." She was lying on the couch smiling to herself and then suddenly sat up, completely out of touch. After a while, she said: "When I was sixteen, I got pregnant, I had a miscarriage. After that, nobody wanted me." I said that maybe she felt that nobody wanted to keep the baby-Debbie. (Debbie in other sessions would tell me that she had had an abortion.) She again seemed lost and after a few moments said she was imagining her grandfather coming to her and asking her to suck his penis. She shook with horror and said how could she think this, she had been very fond of him. I said to her that, a moment before, she had been talking about a baby that was also Debbie being dropped and lost, and perhaps these feelings were too unbearable to stay with, so she had to switch to dirty, sexy thoughts.

Debbie repeatedly immersed herself in ruminations whereby she was both hurt and did hurtful things to others; she was both the victim and the bully. Through her daydreams of sado-masochistic excitement and degrading sexual intercourse, she was, in her confusion, trying to recover a sense of her own value, a sense that had been shattered by her experience of oedipal jealousy and envy. The terrified and perverse excitement of the sado-masochistic phantasies became a way of holding herself together and served as an alternative to the psychic containment she lacked. The hard and painful job of trying to provide her with some kind of thinking containment through therapy so that she can gradually stop turning to addictive, violent daydreams is still in progress.

Tania

For Tania, the unmanageable oedipal conflict centred on her attempts to gain love and attention from a cruel, rejecting, but charismatic internal father at the expense of her mother and her sisters. She was at war with her siblings, both imaginary and real. Tania referred herself to the clinic, at the age of 19 years, following repeated periods of severe depression with suicidal impulses. She was attached to her boyfriend of many years, but this relationship was at risk of breaking down due to the scenes of extreme verbal and physical violence which she would create without apparent cause. We agreed to meet twice a week for psychotherapy.

Since Tania's psychotic breakdown at the age of 16, she had made a number of serious suicidal attempts, which led to her being admitted to a psychiatric hospital where she remained an in-patient for nearly a year. She was the youngest of three sisters. She had described her father as a man who was energetic and full of life. While he was demonstrative in his love for his wife, he was sarcastic and a disciplinarian to the point of cruelty with his daughters. Tania's mother was gentle and unassuming, submissive towards her husband, and unable to protect her daughters from her husband's tyranny. Her own fragility did not leave room for her to be in touch with the girls' feelings. The three sisters were full of hatred for each other. In an atmosphere of bitter competitiveness between them, they all felt deprived of their father's love. In Tania's words: "There was not enough to go round, we were like hungry dogs fighting over a bone."

From her earliest memories, Tania feared that her parents would die. She often went to their room at night to check whether they were still breathing. She described going through various rituals and prayers in order to keep her father alive. She secretly searched her parents' drawers in order to steal money and small objects from her mother. Tania desperately wanted to be loved and valued by her father, but in her therapy she also acknowledged how much she hated him for being so cruel and hard. Tania was 15 when he died suddenly of a heart attack in her presence.

It was following this that she collapsed and had a breakdown.

Tania felt desperately guilty for not having kept her father alive, and she realized that with his death she would never have the chance for him to appreciate or love her. She began to hear his voice calling her towards death. She spent nights in the cemetery and started cutting herself and taking drugs. Her mother refused the sisters' efforts to draw her attention to Tania's state of mind. She would say that her "little girl" would never do such things.

In the therapy, Tania was like a little girl who could easily feel abandoned, and she would quickly fall into a state of despair, seeing herself as worthless, "not good enough", and ultimately unlovable. She had nevertheless a powerful presence, and she was intelligent, defended, and controlling. Tania often expressed herself with lyrical eloquence, but she could become intoxicated by her own words. She gave an impression of great vulnerability but also of a violence ready to explode if she felt criticized or if the control she exercised was challenged. In the transference she felt excluded from the parental couple, which she wanted to destroy and separate at all costs. This was also reflected in her fear in other potential intimate relationships, including her relationship with me. She feared that she would lose control if she allowed herself to become really emotionally involved and therefore dependent. Controlling all her relations was of primary importance to Tania.

In my countertransference, I felt violently controlled by her and at times almost immobilized. The atmosphere could feel threatening. For a long time, I felt I could hardly speak of our relationship, of her need for help, of feelings of helplessness. I felt she would want to hate me, get up, leave and never return. All these feelings needed to be lodged in me: I felt impotent, inadequate, small, excluded. It was only when Tania was more trusting of me and felt that I wouldn't abandon her that I could start talking to her about these feelings and we could think together about the underlying fear that her envy, competitiveness, and possessiveness would destroy us both.

Tania's jealousy, as well as her fear that her devoted boyfriend would betray her, had a delusional quality to it. At the beginning of her therapy, she thought that I was secretly meeting her boyfriend and that we were plotting to get rid of her in order to continue our affair. In several of her dreams, her boyfriend and I were digging her grave. When she believed herself to be abandoned and unloved—for instance, at the end of a session or before the holidays—she felt she was falling into a bottomless pit. This falling image represented not only her feeling of being unheld, but also her sense of destroying everything around her. She would then throw herself into a rage and move into a world of her own, a world of morbid phantasy and omnipotence. Her sense of omnipotence was a frantic defence against the intolerable feeling of having been abandoned. She felt she was no longer dependent on me or on her boyfriend who played such a central role in her life.

At the end of a session, Tania once told me that she thought that "You have teleported me onto a ship and I am now the captain in charge of a headless ship. I march up and down the deck, you [H.D.] get off. I am on my own on an endless journey. The child in me feels cut off and undervalued. Sometimes I go below deck and get drunk". At other times when Tania felt distrustful, she retired to what she called the "dark room", where she sacrificed herself to keep her boyfriend or me alive. With obvious complacency she would then tell herself horrible tales of abandonment, betrayal, and destruction, tales with which she would become intoxicated. She would say: "I make this melancholic drink and get drunk on it. I flatten everything, I smash myself to pieces and I am left with all these pieces. I feel so abandoned." A great deal of work was needed to break through Tania's self-idealization and the notion that self-destructive behaviour was just the consequence of feeling abandoned and undervalued.

In our second year of therapy, Tania reported the following dream: "*I had this baby with me, with no clothes on. It was night and I was dressed in black leather. I was driving a huge motorbike at enormous speed. The baby was at the back. I trusted that the baby was all right.*" A bit later, Tania added: "*The baby was all pink and round, one could have eaten it.*" Tania said that the motorbike made her feel powerful and in control. She continued by telling me that the previous day her boyfriend had taken out his young niece but that she, Tania, had refused to go out with them. She described feeling excluded. She felt that nobody cared about her. She said: "I felt near the edge and got drunk."

Although Tania doesn't appear helpless in her black leather, the baby is in fact naked and vulnerable, and its precarious position at the back of the bike is strongly reminiscent of Tania's previous images of falling. Again, she resorts to omnipotence represented this time by the huge motorbike. Dressed as a Hell's Angel and riding this motorbike, Tania is identifying with a bad but very powerful internal father. No mother is looking after the baby but Tania herself as a reckless Hell's Angel. The joint destructiveness of this dangerously powerful internal father straddled by a Hell's Angel puts at risk Tania's helpless infantile self, as well as her vulnerable baby siblings. The enormous speed of the bike conveys Tania's fascination with omnipotence and a destructiveness of which she was well aware and which at other times manifested itself in the form of her suicidal thoughts.

Tania's violence had an addictive quality. She had not felt contained by her parents but was ill-equipped to face oedipal jealousy. Confronted with such jealousy, she turned to the destructive aspect of her personality, seeking to protect herself from unbearable experiences of extreme helplessness. Only very gradually was Tania more able to contain her destructiveness and to show concern for her objects. In the transference, she began to allow me to be part of a good parental couple taking care of her.

Thomas

Thomas was 17 years old when he was referred to the clinic for panic attacks so severe that they stopped him from going to school. He had become practically house-bound following his first panic attack a year earlier. This attack occurred after he had been looking at photographs of his deceased grandmother when she was young. Several attacks followed a few months later, after taking large quantities of soft drugs with his group of friends. By the time he came to the clinic he felt that his whole world had fallen apart. He was depressed and scared all the time, and he could see little point in life.

Thomas was keen to accept my offer of individual psychotherapy. I saw him for four years, twice a week during the first year and then once weekly for the remaining three. When I first met him, I was shocked by his physical appearance. He was extremely thin, his face was a sickly grey, and his very long, uncombed hair hung down to the middle of his back. Although it was a cold day he wore a skimpy jacket, and there were huge holes in his trousers. He looked like a tramp and gave a deep impression of physical and emotional misery. He seemed to be in a state of complete disintegration. He cried during most of the assessment sessions, telling me how he could not cope, and how everything felt too much. He just wanted to lie down and sleep. At the end of each of these meetings, he begged me not to throw him out.

Gradually, as Thomas recounted his childhood, the events that he felt had precipitated his breakdown emerged. His childhood with his mother, father, and sister (five years younger than him) had been very happy. He described feeling close to his divorced grandmother, whom he had "idolized". As a child he said: "The whole world revolved around me. My mother and my grandmother were part of me, and I looked up to my father. He was strong, always right, he was the leader." Then, when Thomas was about 10 years old, his father left the family for another woman. A few months later his much loved grandmother suddenly died, leaving Thomas haunted for years by the image of her body in the coffin.

Death, ugliness, and a tremendous sense of unfairness and loss seemed to have suddenly invaded Thomas's world. He felt that everything worthwhile had collapsed. It was as if he had lost "his backbone" when his father left, and he said: "When my parents divorced and I was alone with my mother, I felt I had to grow, but I didn't really grow, just inwards, like ingrown toenails." Referring to the loss of his grandmother Thomas said: "My childhood ended when she died and the whole of me died." He described how his mother became out of touch with and persecuted by her children's needs. Although he managed to maintain contact with his father, it was a further blow for him when, shortly after his parents' separation, his father lost his job and remained unemployed. Communication between father and son became difficult and Thomas stopped admiring him. He would often say that at the age of 10 or 11 he was suddenly required to grow up. Meanwhile, his mother had remarried, and Thomas felt unmitigated hatred for his new stepfather. He also talked about his hatred of his grandfather, whom he described as an uneducated, angry, and argumentative person.

For a long time, Thomas used his therapy to pour out his depression, his "*mal de vivre*", and his complaints about a whole range of ailments which included dizziness, sore eyes, exhaustion, and an imaginary brain tumor. In this way he seemed to want to fill me with those feelings. He was lost, drifting aimlessly, depressed, and close to falling apart. But there was also a self-indulgent and omnipotent side to him in which his blaming and raging about all the "shit in the world" had a triumphant and gratifying quality. His moods constantly oscillated between manic elation and depression. I also noted that while he was often self-destructive, in his therapy he could be sensitive and personable. At times, he showed his appreciation that all his feelings had a place with me and that we could begin to think about them together. For a while, Thomas seemed to live between his bed and the therapy room, but he gradually returned to school for a few hours a week and he was able to do an A level in art, despite complaining bitterly of feeling ill all the time.

As well as a deeply ingrained conviction that he was too ill and too fragile to cope with life, Thomas had a deep and intense hatred and contempt for men. He often expressed these feelings in a categorical refusal to be a man. For example, about his stepfather he would say: "My mother sees him as charming, I see some beast. I feel sheer revulsion for him. He is diabolical, a creep, he is wrong, he is evil, he might poison us all." And about men more generally: "I don't feel like a man. Men are macho; men are powerful and strong, but in fact they are stupid. The world is run by men. They become hardened when on their own. The only way for men is to be loved by a woman, it's all they have got. Women are the real power and wisdom." Thomas did not feel at home in his own male body: "My body is not my own. Perhaps it is my father's or somebody else's."

After some time, Thomas resumed his nightlife, which included going to clubs with his friends and drinking. He now stayed off drugs, aware of the danger for him. He talked about feeling part of the crowd and at the same time a complete outsider, pretending to be a "bloke" but feeling old, ugly, and inadequate. He desperately wanted a girlfriend but thought it was too late. Frightened that he would "jump in" and that a relationship would become an obsession, he recalled a previous attempt at a relationship where he had so idealized the girl that he felt his own personality had been quite lost. He was so identified with women that he felt that his feminine attributes were what would attract girls to him. "Everybody's after my hair", he would tell me. "I want to cut it but I may lose my appeal."

Following a Christmas holiday, Thomas described a party where he met Kate. She became his first girlfriend: "I was talking to this girl. We talked and talked in a corner and she told me that I was really nice and asked if she could be my girlfriend. I said no, but I really wanted to tell her that I would love her forever. She asked me to kiss her and I said no and when she asked me why, I told her, because I had to make it clear, 'I am not a man'. She was nice though and said she hoped that I would get over whatever it is that I am going through." Thomas was terrified of being disappointed: "If I kiss someone, I don't know what will happen. I should stop myself. I should save myself from something dangerous like disillusion."

Thomas was longing to immerse himself inside the safety and comfort of the mother of his childhood, now represented by Kate. He feared "something like disillusion", the possibility of being turned away from this sanctuary, just as he had lost the security of an intact family. It was also linked to earlier experiences of being close to his mother as a baby when he had felt that he had sole possession of his mother with no father to think about. Claustrophobic anxieties are often related to very early infantile fears of being trapped inside the mother (Klein, 1946; Meltzer, 1992).

All young children are fascinated by the inside of mother, which is felt to contain the source of goodness and safety. At times, young children really believe, at some level of the mind, that they can get back inside their mother in order to gain safety and comfort. It can also be a way of avoiding the painful experience of being a person separate from mother. For some children and adolescents, this defence can turn into a way of life. But because the child or adolescent is then exposed to the fear of being trapped inside, the refuge turns into a bad place. There is, furthermore, a fear of the revenge from all the rivals (siblings and father) who are felt to be with mother all the time.

In the case of Thomas, the desire to live in phantasy inside his mother seemed to proceed from the experience of a mother who was affectionate but not really available emotionally. This phantasy was meant to allow him to lose himself in a fusion with mother. In reality, it exposed him to the claustrophobic anxiety of retaliation from the father and siblings which led to the panic attacks. In Thomas's mind, men were always cruel bullies. This was why he preferred to see himself as a child or a girl with long hair and why he had to explain to Kate that he was not a man. Despite intense self-doubt and extensive ruminations, Thomas did fall in love with Kate and they had a tender relationship, but when she wanted to make love he was petrified. During a session that I will now describe in detail,

Thomas experienced intense claustrophobic anxieties, and we were able to talk further about the meaning of the panic attacks and the fear of having a close sexual relationship.

Thomas started by saying: "Kate and I have not had sex yet. Whatever I plan doesn't happen. Things happen to me, I'm not in control." I talked about a side of Thomas that felt that having sex meant taking the place of his father and of other rivals, and that this was frightening. He replied that he didn't "want to procreate at all. One should not enlarge the human race". I suggested that this idea made him feel worried and guilty. Thomas said: "It doesn't feel right to talk about it any more, it's wrong, wrong." He became increasingly agitated, adding: "I feel I shouldn't be here. It happens to me all the time. I feel ok then suddenly I have the shock of realizing that things are not what I thought. It's like having a panic attack. You suddenly snap out of what you are doing and you think about things." This, I pointed out, is what seemed to have happened here just now. He agreed, adding: "Yes. Listening to what you are saying, not feeling right about being here." I went further and suggested that he had this feeling that he was describing not only with Kate, but also when he felt close to me, in this room, when we talked together about these intimate matters. He might then feel that he had taken over the father's place with me.

We could then think together about how Thomas felt like an intruder both with me and with Kate. Thomas said: "When I am happy I want to be a father. When I'm sad I feel like I don't deserve to be here, that my being born is like I am an impostor." I talked about his guilt about being born, since he thought that this meant others being wiped out. I suggested that he felt worried and guilty about taking possession of the mother, or me here, and this left no room for the father, or for other siblings, the other "babies". With bitterness, Thomas agreed, saying: "Yes, I'm depriving them—I know what competition is—I'm ok, stuff them, fuck off, I can get all the milk." He added: "You have to look after yourself, because my mum is just a kid. Kill or be killed, this is how people live." Thomas was showing me how, in his mind, he either kills the father and the other "babies" or he is their passive victim and he is killed. Therefore, one has to be tough because there aren't any real parents around.

When Thomas identified with the victim, he said: "That's what I can't get over. I can't ignore everybody's suffering. I should be doing something, I should be Jesus—he died for everyone. He wasn't the son of God, he was an anguished man. He saw all the shit. I feel the same way." Here we could see the omnipotent side of Thomas. He had to rescue all the victims in the world to make up for the fact that he could not believe in the idea of his mother's (or my) capacity to care for him and give him the protection he needed. This lack of trust was particularly marked as we were approaching the summer break.

Talking about having sex with his girlfriend made Thomas, in an almost delusional way, feel as if he had succeeded in getting inside the mother, a thought that, on its own, could induce a panic attack. Sitting in the therapy room and being emotionally close to me made his experience of intrusion feel all the more concrete. His sense that he "shouldn't be here" indicated his fear of the strangeness of the experience. It also indicated his guilt over his ability to take the special place inside mother/me, over and above the father and any other siblings (real or imaginary). His aggressiveness, his need to overcome his rivals, had to be quickly projected somewhere else. In this instance, Thomas projected it all into his mental image of a bad father. This conveniently left Thomas back on the same side as the victim. Finally, in a manic and grandiose manner he saw himself as a Christ-like figure left to repair the damage caused by a sadistic father and rival siblings.

Thomas's urge to intrude and seek refuge in phantasy by being over close to a mother appeared to proceed from a lack of trust in good parents. This lack reflected his experiences in earlier life when his father left home, his grandmother died suddenly, his mother became emotionally unavailable for him, and his new stepfather was felt to be cold and unsupportive. The longing for a "lost paradise" was further fostered by his belief that as a child before his father left, his mother and grandmother had been part of him. His early enmeshment with mother and grandmother is reflected in the way he seemed to lose himself in the first girl he was attracted to, and in the way he longed to feel safe, like a bird in a nest. Moreover, such a non-differentiated early relationship had left him especially fragile in the face of the task of becoming a separate individual.

Thomas's view of the world, of men, and of life in general was highly influenced by his experience of himself as a frightened interloper who longed to creep back into a haven from which he felt excluded. During this period of his therapy, Thomas had reverted to spending most of his time lying in bed or going to clubs, feeling ashamed and under constant threat, rather like a Kafka character.

Then Thomas had a dream that the moon was going to crash into the earth, and that a scientist had told him that this would destroy the earth. This dream seemed to capture powerfully his fear that intercourse with his girlfriend would allow a primitive terror to be realized. The terror was not only the danger of fusion with his mother, but also the end to his lifelong repudiation of the idea of his father's intercourse with his mother, which threatened him with such a feeling of danger. Perhaps the collision of these two entities separated since the origin of the Solar System also represented Thomas's fear that actually to make love with his girlfriend would move him to face the fact that maleness was really and unequivocally part of himself. He feared that this new identity, now including his father, would be fatal to him.

A few weeks later, Thomas and his girlfriend made love. Their relationship seemed to be very tender but also over-dependent and anxious. Thomas had been overwhelmed by the intensity of his feeling and his fear that he would lose himself inside his girlfriend. Behind his fear was indeed the anxiety of a primitive re-awakening of infantile passions with which he was still very much involved, since they had never been properly integrated with his external life. After the holidays, he said: "One side of me is euphoric, happy. The other side is despairing, crushed and everything is falling apart. When I'm in one state of mind I can't remember the other. Sometimes," he said, "I think I'm schizophrenic."

The threat of another breakdown came very near to being realized. Thomas had been accepted at another art school which he now hated. The work was too much, and he felt that he could not cope. He thought that the male teacher criticized him, and he took it badly, saying they were all pigs. At home, he was getting more angry with his mother and her partner, even threatening to kill the stepfather. He dropped out of art school in a state of rage and collapse, and soon afterwards he came to his session in a disintegrated state reminiscent of the beginning of the therapy. He said that he was having a breakdown, that he could not cope, and that he didn't want to go on trying. Instead, he wanted to go to a mental hospital. He cried and complained that he couldn't manage to sleep any more; he was scared and depressed. "I have a hollow core . . . I'm completely screwed up. I forgot that I even love Kate." Thomas was aware that he was in danger of losing all his good feelings, and for several weeks he needed me to hold on to his hope for the future and to some belief that he did, after all, have the strength to overcome this crisis.

Towards the end of the second year of the therapy, Thomas applied to a prestigious art school, this time for a foundation course, and was accepted. A few weeks later, he decided not to take up the offer because he realized he did not want to be an artist. He felt that he had never developed or learned much and that he had wasted his education. He wanted to go back to school and start again, this time to get a real education. "Perhaps," he said, "I will have pleasure in learning." He enrolled in a college to do three A-levels. At the beginning, he had great difficulty since he was not used to concentrating or making an effort. People around him were younger than he, but he was able to settle down. He appreciated his teachers' help and support.

Another crisis came when his relationship with Kate broke down just before she was about to go to university. Although she had found someone else, the actual difficulty seemed to be more to do with having to face the pain of separating. The break up revived all of Thomas's rage, despair, and bitterness. But he did not collapse this time and he and Kate were able eventually to remain friends. Thomas worked hard for his exams, and he took a summer job which required hard physical work. By the end of the summer, he was able to leave London and begin his university career.

There were external factors that helped Thomas to develop and grow. His mother and stepfather did eventually separate, and she found a new partner. Thomas was fond of this new man in his mother's life, who didn't actually live with her. His perception of his grandfather changed, and he could talk with affection about his old-fashioned common sense. They now did gardening together. The degree that Thomas had chosen to do combined essential aspects of his mother's and grandfather's professions. By the time Thomas started college, he had cut his hair to shoulder length and was wearing it neatly in a ponytail. Just before stopping the therapy, he went further and had it cut even shorter. By then he looked like a young man, but his face still betrayed a great sensitivity, bordering on fragility. He expressed deep anxieties about stopping and about how he would cope on his own. But he also conveyed a sense of excitement and adventure.

In one of his last sessions, Thomas was looking forward to starting his new summer job, and he talked about the form-tutor who had helped him to get the job. He felt that his teachers had been very helpful, that they were really "nice men". In his enthusiasm, he added that coming here "was the biggest help". He felt that this was the right time to cut his hair, and he said: "I used to feel that my hair was me."

The restoration of a good image of the father was central to the establishment of Thomas's sexual identity. This image had collapsed when his father had left home and lost his job, but it seems likely that it had always been very fragile. In his adolescence, Thomas had identified with a pathetic and fragile male figure. He projected his rage and violence into bad, "macho" men. Until he was able to integrate his feelings enough, his refusal to identify with men pushed him towards effeminacy, to his view that he was not really a man. This left him only able to identify with girls and women whom he idealized. Accepting that men, like his male teachers and his mother's partner, could be helpful, that firm limits were necessary, further enabled Thomas to internalize a paternal function. He was also able to recognize how the more frightening and predatory aspects of maleness in himself were an essential part of his growing up.

Conclusion

The young people considered here had been unable to meet the demands of adolescence and the transition to adulthood. Debbie's emotional isolation and her sense of being worthless became intolerable in adolescence as she faced school examinations. The surge of sexual preoccupation meant that her jealousy and envy of her peers who represented her mother and sisters was directed to their sexual activity. Tania was shaken to the core by the death of her father, as she had been left with unresolved psychological conflict. The steady relationship that she then managed to establish with her boyfriend had exposed her to extreme jealousy which unleashed storms of destructiveness. The issue for Thomas had been that of developing into a young man capable of achievement and in particular of asserting his sexual identity and establishing a sexual relationship.

These adolescents crossed the frontier into psychotic and borderline states because of an incapacity to withstand psychic pain in the absence of a containing maternal object. Their difficulties were compounded by the introjection of a bad internal father. Debbie's identification with a cruel internal father had resulted in her immersion in a world of sado-masochistic phantasies at such depths that the distinction between phantasy and reality was blurred. As for Tania, she confused strength with an identification with a cruel and violent internal father. She abandoned herself to destructive phantasies and outbursts of violence. In Thomas's internal world, men were brutes and ineffectual failures, while sense and sensibility were confined to girls and women. His internal father was incapable of preventing Thomas from intruding, in phantasy, inside the mother. This resulted in claustrophobic anxieties and panic attacks. Furthermore, this boy's incapacity to identify with a good internal father had contributed to his extreme fragility and left him exposed to psychological disintegration.

For each of these adolescents, progress in the therapy depended on providing them with a combination of containment and firm limit-setting corresponding to a robust parental couple. The task of containment seemed to involve an initial period of time when the therapy was used as a place for pouring out feelings that needed to be processed together. Countertransference communications were crucial throughout therapy fully to appreciate the portrayed horrors of a vivid internal world as well as the impact of a difficult external environment.

The developmental stage of adolescence needs to be appreciated as a time of tremendous upheaval and transition, fraught with pressures to grow up, to perform academically, and often to leave home. In the midst of all of this, and perhaps most significantly, the surge of sexuality at adolescence which causes the reawakening of infantile oedipal phantasies has to be negotiated and worked through in the therapy. Neither Debbie, nor Tania, nor Thomas had the experience of a parent capable of containing their feelings. They were thus very fragile emotionally. Without help, they were unable to process the trauma in their lives: for Debbie, her mother's accident and emotional withdrawal from her; for Tania, her father's death; for Thomas, his parents' separation and his mother's deep depression. While the mother was emotionally unavailable, the father was distant, rejecting, or cruel. Furthermore, these adolescents had projected their own competitive aggressiveness into their father and siblings who were consequently experienced as threatening and monstrous.

Since they had internalized an inadequate parental couple, Debbie, Tania, and Thomas were unable to cope with the anxieties that arose from their oedipal phantasies. They experienced their sexual development as a fight to the death with the malevolent father or as the means to placate and seduce him. In their minds, they formed sado-masochistic relationships in which they were either the father's victim or were identified with his violence. The unconscious phantasy seemed to have been that this deadly struggle took place inside their mother's body. Unable to cope with the anxieties engendered by the violent internal world they were inhabiting, the pressure eventually led these emotionally fragile young people to psychotic breakdown.

The psychotherapy of these three disturbed adolescents has essentially been concerned with containing their extreme anxieties and in this way gradually helping them to resolve their psychotic confusion. Thinking containment, as Bion's work has demonstrated, is a necessary precondition for the establishment of greater integration of the personality and the internalization of good figures upon which emotional development relies.

REFERENCES

Abely, P. (1930). Le signe de miroir dans les psychose et plus specialment dans la démance précoce. *Annals Medico Psychologiques, 1.*

Amar, N., Bayle, G., & Salem, I. (1988). *Formation en psychodrame analytique.* Paris: Dunod.

Anastasopoulos, D., & Tsiantis, J. (1996). Countertransference issues in psychoanalytic psychotherapy with children and adolescents: a brief review. In: J. Tsiantis, A.-M. Sandler, D. Anastasopoulos, & B. Martindale (Eds.), *Countertransference in Psychoanalytic Psychotherapy with Children and Adolescents.* London: Karnac Books.

Andreasen, N. C., & Nardach, J. (1977). Dysmorphophobia: symptom or disease? *American Journal of Psychiatry, 134*: 73–76.

Bach, S., & Schwartz, L. (1972). A dream of the Marquis de Sade: psychoanalytic reflections on narcissistic trauma, decompensation and the reconstruction of a delusional self. *Journal of the American Psychoanalytical Association, 20*: 451–475.

Balier, C. (1985). Une aire thérapeutique en prison. In: A. M. Alléon, O. Morvan, & S. Lebovici (Eds.), *Adolescence Terminée, Adolescence Interminable.* Paris: PUF.

Baranger, M., Baranger, W., & Mom, J. M. (1988). The infantile psychic trauma from us to Freud: pure trauma, retroactivity and reconstruction. *International Journal of Psycho-Analysis, 69*: 113–128.

Benedetti, G. (1964). *Der psychisch leidende und seine Welt*. Stuttgart: Hippokrates.

Benedetti, G. (1983). *Psychosentherapie*. Stuttgart: Hippokrates.

Bergmann, M., & Jucovy, M. (Eds.) (1982). *Generations of the Holocaust*. New York: Basic Books.

Bessel, A., & Van der Kolk, S. (1985). Adolescent vulnerability to post-traumatic stress disorder. *Psychiatry, 48*: 365–370.

Bick, E. (1968). The experience of the skin in early object relations. *International Journal of Psycho-Analysis, 49*: 484–486. [Also in M. Harris & E. Bick, *Collected Papers of Martha Harris and Esther Bick*. Strathtay: Clunie Press, 1987.]

Bion, W. (1959). Attacks on linking. In: *Second Thoughts* (pp. 93–109). London: Heinemann, 1967. [Reprinted London: Karnac Books, 1984.]

Bion, W. R. (1962a). *Learning from Experience*. London: Heinemann. [Reprinted London: Karnac Books, 1984.]

Bion, W. R. (1962b). A theory of thinking. *International Journal of Psycho-Analysis, 43*: 306–310. [Also in *Second Thoughts*, London: Heinemann, 1967; reprinted London: Karnac Books, 1984.]

Bion, W. R. (1963). *Elements of Psycho-Analysis*. London: Heinemann. [Reprinted London: Karnac Books, 1989.]

Bion, W. R. (1977). *Seven Servants*. Northvale, NJ: Jason Aronson.

Bion, W. R. (1979). *The Dawn of Oblivion. A Memoir of the Future, Book 3*. London: Karnac Books, 1991.

Blankenburg, W. (1982). Körper und Leib. *Schweizer Archiv für Neurologie und Psychiatrie, 131* (3): 13–39.

Blos, P. (1962). *On Adolescence*. New York: Free Press.

Blos, P. (1967). The second individuation process of adolescence. In: *The Adolescent Passage*. New York: International Universities Press, 1982.

Blos, P. (1968). Character formation in adolescence. *Psychoanalytic Study of the Child, 23*: 245–263.

Blum, H. (1986). The concept of the reconstruction of trauma. In: A. Rothstein (Ed.), *The Reconstruction of Trauma: Its Significance in Clinical Work*. New York: International Universities Press.

Botella, C., & Botella, S. (1984). L'homosexualité inconsciente et le dynamique du double en séance. *Revue Française de Psychanalyse, 47* (3): 687–708.

Brandell, J. (1992). Countertransference phenomena in the psychotherapy of children and adolescents. In: J. Brandell (Ed.), *Countertansference in Psychotherapy with Children and Adolescents*. New York: Jason Aronson.

Brusset, B. (1990). Les vicissitudes d'une déambulation addictive (essai métapsychologique). *Revue Française de Psychanalyse, 54* (3): 671–687.

Casement, P. (1987). The experience of trauma in the transference. In: J. Klauber (Ed.), *Illusion and Spontaneity in Psychoanalysis* (pp. 78–98). London: Free Association Books.

Chabert, C. (1997). Féminin mélancolique. *Adolescence, 30*: 47–57.

Chasseguet-Smirgel, J. (1975). *L'ideal de moi.* Paris: Tschou.

Chasseguet-Smirgel, J. (1986). *Sexuality and Mind: The Role of Father and the Mother in the Psyche.* New York: International Universities Press.

Connolly, F. H., & Gipson, M. (1978). Dysmorphophobia—a long term study. *British Journal of Psychiatry, 132*: 568–570.

Cooper, A. (1986). Toward a limited definition of trauma. In: A. Rothstein (Ed.), *The Reconstruction of Trauma.* Workshop Series of the American Psychoanalytic Association. New York: International Universities Press.

de Saussure, J. (1982). Dreams and dreaming in relation to trauma in childhood. *International Journal of Psycho-Analysis, 63* (2): 167–175.

De Wind, E. (1984). Some implications of former massive traumatization upon the actual analytic process. *International Journal of Psycho-Analysis, 65* (3): 273–281.

Dorpat, T. L. (1990). Female homosexuality: an overview. In: C. W. Socarides & V. D. Volkan (Eds.), *The Homosexualities* (pp. 111–139). Madison, WI: International Universities Press.

Federn, P. (1952). *Ego Psychology and the Psychoses.* New York: Basic Books. [Reprinted London: Karnac Books, 1977.]

Ferenczi, S. (1924). Versuch einer Genitaltheorie. In: *Schriften zur Psychoanalyse.* Frankfurt: Fischer, 1970.

Freud, S. (1895d) with Breuer, J. *Studies on Hysteria. S.E., 2.*

Freud, S. (1911c [1910]). Psycho-analytic notes on an autobiograhical account of a case of Paranoia (Dementia paranoides). *S.E., 12*: 1–79.

Freud, S. (1914d). On the history of the psychoanalytic movement. *S.E., 14*: 7–66.

Freud, S. (1914g). Remembering, repeating, and working-through. *S.E., 12*: 147–156.

Freud, S. (1916d). Some character-types met with in psycho-analytic work. *S.E., 14*: 311–336.

Freud, S. (1918b [1914]). From the history of an infantile neurosis. *S.E.,* 17: 1–122.

Freud, S. (1919h). The "uncanny". *S.E., 17:* 217–253.

Freud, S. (1920g). *Beyond the Pleasure Principle. S.E., 18*: 1–66.

Freud, S. (1925h). Negation. *S.E., 19*: 235–240.

Freud, S. (1925f). Preface to A. Aichhorn's *Verwahrloste Jugend. S.E.,* 19.

Freud, S. (1926d [1925]). *Inhibition, Symptoms and Anxiety. S.E., 20*: 77–174.

Furst, S. (1986). Psychic trauma and its reconstruction with particular reference to post childhood trauma. In: A. Rothstein (Ed.), *The Reconstruction of Trauma: Its Significance in Clinical Work.* New York: International Universities Press.

Gillibert, J. (1985). *Le psychodrame de la psychoanalyse.* Paris: Champ Vallon.

Glasser, M. (1979). Some aspects of the role of aggression in perversion. In: I. Rosen (Ed.), *Sexual Deviation.* London: Oxford University Press.

Glick, R., & Meyers, D. (1988). Introduction. In: E. Glick & D. Meyers (Eds.), *Masochism: Current Psychoanalytic Perspectives.* Hillsdale, NJ: Analytic Press.

Green, A. (1980). La mère morte. In: *Narcissisme de vie, narcissisme de mort* (pp. 222–254). Paris: Minuit. [In English, "The dead mother", in: *On Private Madness,* 1986. Reprinted London: Karnac Books, 1977.]

Green, A. (1982). Après-coup, l'archaïque. *Nouvelle Revue de Psychanalyse, 26*: 195–215.

Green, A. (Ed.) (1995). *La causalité psychique. Entre nature et culture.* Paris: Odile Jacob.

Greenacre, P. (1967). The influence of infantile trauma on genetic patterns. In: S. Furst (Ed.), *Psychic Trauma* (pp. 108–153). New York: International Universities Press.

Grünberger, B. (1971). *Le narcissisme. Essais de psychanalyse.* Paris: Payot.

Hinshelwood, R. D. (1989). *A Dictionary of Kleinian Thought.* London: Free Association Books. [2nd edition, 1991.]

Jackson, M. (1992). Learning to think about schizoid thinking. In: A. Werbart & J. Cullberg (Eds.), *Psychotherapy of Schizophrenia: Facilitating and Obstructive Factors* (pp. 37–49). Proceedings of the Xth International Symposium for the Psychotherapy of Schizophrenia. Oslo: Scandinavian University Press.

Jacobson, E. (1959). Depersonalization. *Journal of the American Psychoanalytical Association, 7*: 581–610.

Jeammet, P. (1992). La thérapie bifocale. *Revue Adolescence, 10* (2): 371–383.

Jeammet, P. (1994). Adolescence et processus de changement. In: D. Widlöcher (Ed.), *Traité de psychopathologie* (pp. 687–726). Paris: PUF.

Jeammet, P., & Chabert, C. (1998). A psychoanalytical approach to eating disorders: the role of dependency. In: A. H. Esman (Ed.), *Adolescent Psychiatry. The Annals of the American Society for Adolescent Psychiatry*, 22: 59–84.

Keats, J. (1817). *Letters of John Keats*, edited by R. Gittings. Oxford: Oxford University Press, 1987.

Kelman, H. (1946). The traumatic syndrome. *American Journal of Psychoanalysis, 6:* 12–19.

Kestemberg, E., & Jeammet, P. (1981). Le psychodrame psychoanalytique: technique, spécificité, indications. *Psychothérapies, 2:* 85–87.

Kestemberg, E., & Jeammet, P. (1987). *Le psychodrame psychanalytique.* Paris: PUF.

Khan, M. M. R. (1974). The concept of cumulative trauma. In: M. M. R. Khan (Ed.), *The Privacy of the Self* (pp. 42–58). London: Hogarth Press. [Reprinted London: Karnac Books, 1996.]

Khan, M. M. R. (1983). *Hidden Selves.* London: Hogarth Press. [Reprinted London: Karnac Books, 1987.]

Klein, M. (1923). The role of the school in the libidinal development of the child. In: *Love, Guilt and Reparation and Other Works 1921–1945: The Writings of Melanie Klein, Vol. 1* (pp. 59–76). London: Hogarth Press, 1975. [Reprinted London: Karnac Books, 1992.]

Klein, M. (1946). Notes on some schizoid mechanisms. In: *Envy and Gratitude and Other Works 1946–1963: The Writings of Melanie Klein, Vol. 3* (pp. 1–24). London: Hogarth Press, 1975. [Reprinted London: Karnac Books, 1993.]

Kohut, H. (1971). *The Analysis of the Self.* London: Hogarth Press.

Kohut, H. (1977). *The Restoration of the Self.* New York: International Universities Press.

Krell, H., & Okin, R. (1984). Countertransference issues in child abuse and neglect cases. *American Journal of Forensic Psychiatry, 5* (1): 7–16.

Krystal, H. (1971). Psychotherapy after massive traumatization. In: H. Krystal & W. G. Niederand (Eds.), *Psychic Traumatization* (pp. 223–229). Boston, MA: Little, Brown.

Laufer, M., & Laufer, M. E. (1984). *Adolescence & Developmental Breakdown.* New Haven, CT: Yale University Press. [Reprinted London: Karnac Books, 1996.]

Lebovici, S., Diatkine, R., & Kestemberg, E. (1958). Bilan de dix ans de pratique psychodramatique chez l'enfant et l'adolescent. *Le Psychiatrie de L'enfant, 1* (2): 63–180.

Le Guen, C. (1982). The trauma of interpretation as history repeating itself. *International Journal of Psycho-Analysis, 63* (3): 321–330.

Mack Brunswick, R. (1929). Ein Nachtrag zu Freuds "Geschichte einer infantilen Neurose". *Internationale Zeitschrift für Psychoanalyse, 15* (1): 1–44.

Mahler, M. S., Pine, F., & Bergman, A. (1975). *The Psychological Birth of the Human Infant*. New York: Basic Books.

Marohn, R. C. (1994). "Psychoanalytic perspectives on adolescent violence." Paper presented at the 13th Congress I.A.C.A.P.A.P., San Francisco, CA.

Marohn, R. C., Dalle Molle, D., McCarter, E., & Linn, D. (1980). *Juvenile Delinquents. Psychodynamic Assessment and Hospital Treatment*. New York: Brunner/Mazel.

Marvasti, J. (1986). Psychotherapy with abused children and adolescents. In: S. Brandell (Ed.), *Countertansference in Psychotherapy with Children and Adolescents*. New York: Jason Aronson.

Masterson, J. F. (1971). Diagnosis and treatment of the borderline syndrome in adolescence. *Confrontations Psychiatriques, 7*: 125–155.

Masterson, J. F., & Rinsley, D. B. (1975). The borderline syndrome: the role of the mother in the genesis and psychic structure of the borderline personality. *International Journal of Psycho-Analysis, 56*: 163–177.

Matte Blanco, I. (1975). *The Unconcious as Infinite Sets*. London: Duckworth. [Reprinted London: Karnac Books, 1998.]

McDougall, J. (1986). Parent loss. In: A. Rothstein (Ed.), *The Reconstruction of Trauma*. Workshop Series of the American Psychoanalytic Association. New York: International Universities Press.

Medri, G. (1983). Die wechselseitige Identifikation als Grundstruktur der therapeutischen Beziehung zum Psychotiker. In: G. Benedetti (Ed.), *Psychosentherapie* (pp. 81–110). Stuttgart: Hippokrates.

Meltzer, D. (1971). Sincerity. In: *Sincerity and Other Works*, edited by A. Hahn. London: Karnac Books, 1994.

Meltzer, D. (1975). Adhesive identification. *Contemporary Psycho-Analysis, 11*: 289–310. [Also in: *Sincerity and Other Works*, edited by A. Hahn. London: Karnac Books, 1994.]

Meltzer, D. (1978). A note on introjective processes. In: *Sincerity and Other Works*, edited by A. Hahn. London: Karnac Books, 1994.

Meltzer, D. (1992). *The Claustrum, An Investigation of Claustrophobic Phenomena*. Perth: Clunie Press.

Morselli, E. (1886). Sulla dismorfobia e sulla tafefobia. *Bolletino della R. Academia di Genova, 6*: 110–119.

Munro, A. (1980). Monosymptomatic hypochondriacal psychosis. *British Journal of Hospital Medicine*: 34–37.

Muses, R. (1978). Adult psychic trauma: the question of early predisposition and some detailed mechanisms. *International Journal of Psycho-Analysis, 59*: 353–363.

Neubauer, P. (1980). The life cycle as indicated by the nature of the transference in the psychoanalysis of children. *International Journal of Psycho-Analysis, 61*: 137–144.

Novelletto, A. (1986). Crimini adolescenti e fantasia di recupero maturativo. *Psichiatria dell'Infanzia e Adolescenza, 53*: 287–292.

Novelletto, A. (1988). Crimes d'adolescents et fantasme de réalisation magique de maturité. *Adolescence, 6* (1): 185–199.

Pao, P.-N. (1979). *Schizophrenic Disorders: Theory and Treatment from a Psychodynamic Point of View*. New York: International University Press.

Pessoa, F. (1977). The child was playing. In: *Obra Poética* (p. 510). Rio de Janeiro: Ed. Nova Aguilar.

Pestalozzi, J. (1988). *Zur Problematik der Dysmorfofobie bei Adoleszenten*. Ph.D. thesis, University of Basel.

Pestalozzi, J. (1996). Psychotische Übertragung als Chance. *Kinderanalyse, 4* (1): 1–54.

Pontalis, J.-B. (1981). Non, deux fois non. *Nouvelle Revue de Psychanalyse, 24*: 53–73.

Rosenfeld, H. A. (1966). *Psychotic States: A Psychoanalytical Approach*. New York: International Universities Press. [Reprinted London: Karnac Books, 1998.]

Rosenfeld, H. A. (1971). Contribution to the psychopathology of psychotic states. In: E. Bott Spillius (Ed.), *Melanie Klein Today, Vol. 1* (pp. 117–137). London: Routledge, 1988.

Rosenfeld, H. A. (1987). *Impasse and Interpretation*. London: Tavistock.

Rothstein, A. (1986). Conclusion: In: A. Rothstein (Ed.), *The Reconstruction of Trauma*. Workshop Series of the American Psychoanalytic Association. New York: International Universities Press.

Roussillon, R. (1991). Epreuve "d'actualité" et "épreuve de réalité dans le face à face psychanalytique". *Revue Française de Psychanalyse, 55* (3): 581–596.

Sandler, J. (1989). Trauma, strain and development. In: J. Sandler (Ed.), *From Safety to Superego* (pp. 127–141). London: Karnac Books.

Sandler, J., Dreher, A. V., & Drew, S. (1991). An approach to conceptual research in psychoanalysis illustrated by consideration of psychic trauma. *International Journal of Psycho-Analysis, 18*: 133–141.

Schilder, P. (1935). *The Image and the Appearance of the Human Body.* New York: International University Press, 1950.

Searles, H. F. (1965). *Collected Papers on Schizophrenia and Related Subjects.* London: Hogarth Press. [Reprinted London: Karnac Books, 1986.]

Sechehaye, M. A. (1951). *Symbolic Realization.* New York: International Universities Press.

Segal, H. (1957). Notes on symbol formation & postscript to notes on symbol formation. In: *The Work of Hanna Segal: A Kleinian Approach to Clinical Practice.* London: Free Association Books, 1986. [Reprinted London: Karnac Books, 1988.]

Segal, H. (1975). A psycho-analytic approach to the treatment of schizophrenia. In: *The Work of Hanna Segal: A Kleinian Approach to Clinical Practice.* London: Free Association Books, 1986. [Reprinted London: Karnac Books, 1988.]

Selvini, M. P. (1967). Contribution à la psychopathologie du vécu corporel. *Evolution Psychiatrique, 32* (1): 150–173.

Sprince, M. J. (1988). Experiencing and recovering transitional space. In: H. J. Schwartz (Ed.), *Bulimia: Psychoanalytic Treatment and Theory* (pp. 73–88). New York: International University Press.

Stone, L. (1961). *The Psychoanalytic Situation.* Madison, WI: International Universities Press.

Terr, L. (1983). Time sense following psychic trauma: a clinical study of ten adults and twenty children. *American Journal of Orthopsychiatry, 53* (2): 244–261.

Terr, L. (1985). Psychic trauma in children and adolescents. *Psychiatric Clinics of North America, 8*: 815–835.

Terr, L. (1987). What happens to early moments of trauma? *American Academy of Child and Adolescent Psychiatry, 1*: 96–104.

Terr, L. (1991). Childhood traumas: an outline and an overview. *American Journal of Psychiatry, 1*: 10–20.

Tonnesman, M. (1980). Adolescent re-enactment, trauma and reconstruction. *Journal of Child Psychotherapy, 6*: 21–44.

Tracey, N. (1991). The psychic space in trauma. *Journal of Child Psychotherapy, 17* (2): 29–43.

Ulman, R. B., & Brothers, D. (1988). *The Shattered Self: A Psycho-Analytic Study of Trauma.* Hillsdale, NJ: Analytic Press.

Volkan, V. D. (1976). *Primitive Internalized Object Relations.* New York: International Universities Press.

Widlöcher, D. (1995). Pour une métapsychologie de l'écoute psychanalytique. *Revue Française de Psychanalyse, numéro spécial Congrès: Métapsychologie, Ecoute et Transitionnalité, 59*: 1721–1786.

Williams, A. H. (1983). *Nevrosi e Delinquenza*. Rome: Borla.

Winnicott, D. W. (1967). Mirror-role of mother and family in child development. In: *Playing and Reality* (pp. 111–118). London: Tavistock, 1971.

Winnicott, D. W. (1971). *Playing and Reality*. London: Routledge.

Woolf, V. (1928). *A Room of One's Own*. Harmondsworth: Penguin, 1945.

INDEX